THE PORCUPINE DILEMMA

By Leopold Bellak

DEMENTIA PRAECOX: THE PAST DECADE'S WORK AND PRESENT STATUS, 1948

PROJECTIVE PSYCHOLOGY, editor and contributor with Lawrence Abt, 1950

MANIC DEPRESSIVE PSYCHOSIS AND ALLIED DISORDERS, 1952

THE PSYCHOLOGY OF PHYSICAL ILLNESS, editor and contributor, 1952

THE TAT AND THE CAT IN CLINICAL USE, 1954

SCHIZOPHRENIA: A REVIEW OF THE SYNDROME, editor and contributor with P. K. Benedict, 1958

CONCEPTUAL AND METHODOLOGICAL PROBLEMS IN PSYCHOANALYSIS, editor, conference chairman, and contributor, 1959

MYOKINETIC PSYCHODIAGNOSIS, co-editor, American edition, 1960

CONTEMPORARY EUROPEAN PSYCHIATRY, editor, 1961

A HANBOOK OF COMMUNITY PSYCHIATRY AND COMMUNITY MENTAL HEALTH, editor and contributor, 1964

EMERGENCY PSYCHOTHERAPY AND BRIEF PSYCHOTHERAPY, with Leonard Small, 1965

THE BROAD SCOPE OF PSYCHOANALYSIS: SELECTED PAPERS OF LEOPOLD BELLAK, edited by Donald Spence, 1969

THE SCHIZOPHRENIC SYNDROME, editor and contributor with Laurence Loeb, 1969

PROGRESS IN COMMUNITY MENTAL HEALTH, Vol. I, editor and contributor with Harvey Barten, 1969

THE
Porcupine
Dilemma

Reflections on the
Human Condition

LEOPOLD BELLAK, 1916–

THE CITADEL PRESS • New York

To the Danish people, who have shown
by their humanity and toughness during World War II
and their daily lives
that they may have solved
"the porcupine dilemma"
better than most other people

Copyright © 1970 by C.P.S., Inc.
Published by
Citadel Press, Inc.
222 Park Avenue South
New York, N. Y. 10003
A subsidiary of Lyle Stuart, Inc.

Library of Congress Catalog Card No. 72-110384
ISBN 0-8065-0223-1

MANUFACTURED IN THE UNITED STATES OF AMERICA

Contents

I. The World We Made

1

Introduction:
The World of Porcupines and Men

ONE WINTRY DAY a couple of chilled porcupines huddled together for warmth. They found that they pricked each other with their quills; they moved apart and were again cold. After much experimentation, the porcupines found the distance at which they gave each other some warmth without too much sting.

This striking fable was told by Arthur Schopenhauer, the moody philosopher of pessimism. It lends itself well to consideration of human comfort in intimacy. How close can we get without interfering with each other? How much warmth do we need? How can we live together without hurting each other too much? That is the *porcupine dilemma*. It appears in the overcrowding of our cities. It is part of the increased interaction produced by evermore travel, communication media, economic, and political interdependence. What happens in a remote desert of

China has an effect on lives in Des Moines, Iowa, and in Albania.

The porcupine dilemma has increased in intensity because more of us affect each other more often. The obvious remedy—more distance—is sometimes not possible. At other times it is not desirable because the resulting impersonalization leaves too little human warmth.

The amount of total "quill input" into each of us could be stated as the *Porcupine Index*. Since the actual amount of input desired, or found bearable, differs in individuals, the porcupine index is not only a measure of input like a voltmeter reading, but also of certain personality characteristics.

Schematically, the P. I. could be defined as P. I. = number of stimuli $\times$ intensity $\times$ duration, each rated from 1 to 10. The term *stimuli* has the advantage of being able to refer either to human conduct or to sounds, light, and the like. Also, it sounds satisfyingly scientific.

In our unsure society, both the number of human contacts and the amount of inanimate input is on the rise. On the subway, buses, airplanes, we meet more people in more ways than in the Victorian age, or twenty years ago, or five years ago. Not only do we meet and interact with more people in person, but also through newspapers, radio, and television. Via communication satellites, there is more *instant* interaction as well—consider for example the international spread of the student revolts. In this broad sense, the total personal stimulus input has grown tremendously. With it, the Porcupine Dilemma —as well as attempts to solve it—has also increased.

2

Hippies, Communes, and the Rousseau Delusion as Attempts to Solve the Porcupine Dilemma

HIPPIES PREACH LOVE, not war; they don't mean only the war of guns, but also the fight for success. Why compete, why knock your brains out to get ahead? They try for a solution exactly opposite to the extreme of the junior executive who sells himself for soap and status.

Henry Miller was one of the important forerunners of the hippie movement. A successful banker, he decided to do away with the detours to pleasure. He traveled, he loved, he lived the simple life. He also found happiness in relative seclusion in Big Sur, and the hippies have followed suit.

I would venture to say that, among other things, Miller and his followers felt especially the discomfort of the quills of competition, the lack of warmth and love and immediacy of our culture. They decided to do away with their personal armor and arms and find warmth without the conventional intermediaries.

The modern communes now springing up all over the United States are also conceived as an answer of similar nature. Let us forgo the struggle of our society, return to cultivating the soil and making our own apparel, and live by a code that permits us proximity and loving warmth without strife. Thus, many a professional raises chickens by the book and plants staple foods like a laboratory experiment.

The idea of such communes is not a new one, and the need to avoid the evil fangs of civilization was also at the root of the old ones. Tax-free communities, property sharing, making one's own implements, and generally living the simple and unaggressive life were also the marks of those ventures.

Thoreau and, before him, Rousseau are prime exponents of this attempt to deal with the complexities of our social relations. Rousseau spoke of the Noble Savage. He felt that the progress of the sciences contributed to the corruption of man. He believed that laws were a device of oppressors to maintain their grip. Though he did not advocate collective ownership, his doctrines had a decided influence on the development of socialism.

Then, as now, a feeling of being overwhelmed by the increasing complexity of science and our social structure was the mainspring of attempts to take the sting out of it by reverting to a more egalitarian, less hierarchical, simpler way of life.

Rousseau was a man with a very thin skin, like our present-day hippies. He found human relations almost intolerable, was quite obviously paranoid, and quarreled sooner or later with all his friends and benefactors, thinking them to be in league with his other enemies. Quite often he had to move to put some physical distance between himself and people he felt had come too close for comfort.

Hippies are generally more pacific than Rousseau, who liked to insult everybody. The recent Music and Arts Festival at Woodstock brought 300,000 young people, mostly of some hippie persuasion, together. *The New York Times* reported as one of the amazing facts that under frustrating and difficult circumstances no violence occurred at all. *It is a safe bet that 300,000 devout aldermen would not have done as well.*

Of course, hippies and much of our youth have access to drugs as a distancing device and anesthetic. When reality becomes too unpleasant, when proximity to others becomes too hard to bear, pot or some other vehicle for a trip is the ultimate in isolation, comparable only to psychotic withdrawal.

Rousseau was the first of the romanticists, influencing many of the outstanding writers, social theorists, politicians, and educators as diverse as Goethe, Tolstoy, Robespierre, and the famous Swiss educator, Pestalozzi.

It is not unreasonable to consider him the forefather of the hippies and to speak of his main propositions as the "Rousseau Delusion": the persistent belief, largely held against evidence to the contrary, that we can turn the clock back socially, scientifically, and technically in order to have a better life.

Surely, the excesses of our civilization, the senseless

arms race toward destruction, the keeping up with the Joneses, and the pretentions of the righteous make Rousseau and the hippies very attractive and appealing alternatives. The trouble is that one extreme is apparently not the best answer to the other extreme.

As Rousseau did in his personal life, communes soon find that they bring their porcupine problems with them. The only question is how long it takes before such difficulties break up their dream. Rarely does it take more than a few years.

Freud had a good deal to say about civilization and its discontent. He too felt that our increasingly complex lives force us into such long detours in order to obtain some pleasure, some satisfaction when the strain becomes very severe. Before the current social changes, adolescents who were of age biologically had to wait until they were self-supporting, respectable members of the community before they could engage in the sexual behavior they were better equipped for than their elders. School, diploma, licenses, and all the other demands of civilization require great frustration tolerance. The Guild system was indeed designed to protect the old incumbents against the young have-nots. However, Freud also pointed out that civilization is largely a result of and dependent upon some of the delay in the various gratifications. Typically, in cultures where coconut trees and bananas provide immediate satiation of hunger, and where the nearest bush makes possible gratification of sexual desires, atomic energy, for better and for worse, has not been developed.

The Rousseau Delusion is not limited to hippies by any means. There are businessmen who become priests out of similar motives. There are other prime exponents of our competitive society who dream of changing to a simple life, and some even do it. There is the desire for a farm in even more people than those who can afford one to take refuge in on weekends. It is heartwarming, amusing, and heartbreaking to see highpowered executives, politicians, and other cutthroats revel in dirty dungarees and even dirtier feet on places as diverse as Martha's Vineyard, Fire Island, Bucks County, or Wyoming, proclaiming that this is the real life. There they feel they have washed off their pretenses, their voraciousness, and vicious maneuvers to stay alive and ahead of the other fellow. In solitude they lick their wounds from hand-to-hand combat.

For there is hardly a person who does not feel that daily civilized life is just too much. In the words of the Broadway musical, *"Stop the World, I Want to Get Off."*

The favorite fantasy for getting off is probably the idea of becoming a beachcomber. The plain life must be the good life—sun, water, no possessions. In the case of a male, throw in some outdated notions of barebreasted maidens in Hawaii, on Bali, Samoa, Tahiti. Forsake the fleshpots of our electronic world and settle for the simple pleasures because the civilized world keeps us so busy fulfilling obligations and paying taxes that there never seems a time for enjoying the basic pleasures.

The fantasy must predate electronics because the notion of paradise has all the ingredients. Certainly the heathen paradise of the Greeks had all their sensuous pleasures. The Teutonic heaven was just a little heavier, as one might expect, but basically not different. Walküren, shaped like Brünhilde in Wagner's opera, would heft giant tumblers of nectar for the warrior who got away from the earthly battles.

Competitive striving tends to make us all feel the other people's proximity too much. Keeping up with or ahead of progress is wearing. It is cumbersome because it takes real energy and also because it induces emotional conflict, anger, and guilt.

That anger and guilt often have early roots. A boy especially starts out life by first emulating his father and then wanting to outdo him. Find a man who wants to give it all back to the Indians, and I'll show you a man who had particularly strong conflicts about competing with his father. The closer he gets to a goal of achievement, the more often he'll think of getting out of the race. Maybe he would just open a little country store or run a gas pump in a small village rather than a corporation. To run a corporation, he would have to elbow another man aside, most likely an older man, and that is too much like getting father out of the way. Or, to get back to the old Greeks, it is a little too much like challenging the gods, who might then turn in wrath.

There also seems to be something dirty-soft in electric blankets, split-level houses, and canned food. Some men get this feeling out of their system by occasional hunting or fishing trips. Getting their feet wet and their derrière cold at the morning rites gives them a clean feeling of being the salt of the earth. A simple, insufficiently-cooked meal over a Sterno fire makes them feel whole and sound again, like men, not organization cogs or even wheels.

Flight to a tropical "paradise" used to be an answer

for some. Somerset Maugham seems to have run across a good many of them.

The Rousseau Delusion is attractive, inadequate and all pervasive. In art, the Delusion leads to nihilism sold as sophistication. The scribblings of an ape are only the final reduction of the idea that primitivism is bliss. On the way, excessively abstracted art leads to symbolism which fails to communicate. To say that symbolic art has individual meaning simply means a breakdown in human relations like the unrelatedness in rock and roll dancing. At best, human relations in discotheques are on the level of "the collective monologue" which Piaget describes as a stage in the development of small children. Before they are able to exchange words meaningfully with each other, they stand in small groups talking to themselves, but not responsively to each other.

In psychology and psychotherapy, the reductionism to absurd primitivity takes the place of encounter groups of various forms. Instead of relearning painstakingly the *painful* distortions of human relations acquired in childhood, direct expression of the need for warmth is supposed to lead to changes by combustion. Not too different from the magic of laying on hands, this magic of encounters proposes to lead to restructuration and improvement of our terribly complex society by spontaneous exchange, touching and even nudity. A partial truth once more beclouds the bigger issue. Of course our lives are too fraught with formulas, with inhibitions with indirection. A frigid, overcontrolled businessman may find spontaneous expression a great relief, and an hysterical woman some fulfillment in acting out her childish needs. The carryover ef-

11

fect to the world of everyday living in our society is minimal. The chances of transferring the social structure of Big Sur to Manhattan and Moscow are very small.

In education, a return to a primitive lack of structure will not prepare children for the ambiguities and frustrations of modern society. Affective education proposes to substitute passion for instruction, as the Rousseau Delusion would substitute ecstasy for insight in therapy. Surely, teaching by computer and televised teachers is woefully inanimate, but shared emotional experience is not an adequate substitute. Much more careful thought will have to be given to education in our too quickly evolving world than is represented by either of these extremes.

We are stuck with a world that has evolved intricate means of communication, that threatens to pollute itself into oblivion, or bomb itself to hell, or overpopulate itself into starvation. It is a frightening image, but to take to the trees again is a delusion, not an answer that will be accepted or could solve the problems. Most of the time Rousseau knew that, for his *contrat social* was an attempt to deal rationally with world problems that could not be met by romantic means.

Our lives may well be choked by gadgets, walled in by laws, and filled with obstacles to any kind of gratification. Yet, within the apparently inescapable framework of our technical civilization, a direct route to gratification is not likely to be an answer for more than an occasional eccentric. What is more, most of us need more complex gratifications than the simple life provides. The path from A to B for gratification seems to lack real enticement, whether B is food, or shelter, or love.

The hippie movement, the youth revolt, have some real points to make. Beards and tattered dungarees are good as statements of intent and sentiment: there is too much detour behavior, too much emphasis on material goods, too much value attached to combativeness. They are understandable ways of protesting an overly patriarchial society which exploits youth as one of the minorities. In their stance, hippies ridicule successfully and appropriately concepts of machismo, of manliness, which went out with the frontier days. There are no heroic stances vis-à-vis the H-bomb. In that sense they are lineal derivatives of the differences in attitude between the First World War and the Second. In the First World War flag waving and singing accompanied the ideas of showing the Boches, of fighting for the Kaiser, of dying for the Tsar, of making the world safe for democracy. In the Second World War, the democratic armies saw it as a grim job of exterminating the Nazi menace, when they saw it at all. After the First World War there was an international youth movement against war, and Vietnam seems to have taken up where it was interrupted by Hitler.

Even the cultural form of youth protest is not new. Social democratic European youth did not wear dungarees, but they wore sport shirts rather than collars and ties —and thought ballroom dancing a bourgeois sneakiness of sexual expression.

It is too easy, though, to mistake forms for substance. Open shirts and flowers are not sufficient to deal with the complexities of our world. They are a beginning. We may do away with dispensable detour behavior, but much of it is indispensable. People who dream of getting away to

13

the simple life suffer from the *delusion* that there is an attainable state of bliss. To a certain extent, such a delusion is vital, an integral part of living. To join the Rousseau delusion to the one of an attainable state of bliss is likely to be ineffective and lead to disaster. It is the result of fear and a lack of a frame of reference.

What is essential is a careful reexamination of what we need to live in the world we have made. Youth must add its voice in the world councils. It must learn, however, that in personal life as well as in international life there are no easy solutions, only detours, because ours is an intricate road with stop lights, bypasses, and other devices necessary to avoid crashing into each other.

In one's personal life the detours often are the scenic road. Making love rather than going to college may be a little like taking the highway from A to B. It may be faster and offer less discomfort, but it may miss most of the beauty. Gourmets probably do better than gourmands. Or as the airlines say—getting there is half the fun.

3

On the Ways of Eggheads, Squareheads, and Fatheads

AS THE MARGIN FOR ERROR DECREASES THERE
IS LESS ROOM FOR A LUNATIC FRINGE

THE BATTLE between eggheads and squareheads is one of the oldest of mankind. Akatmemnon doubtlessly was an egghead fighting the Egyptian priest-bureaucrats; the great Athenians were playing that role opposite the rigid Spartans. It is the battle between the creative and the executive, between philosophers and ward heelers, between the toughminded and the tenderminded that James wrote about, or the *klassiche* and the *romantische* that Schiller mentioned, or even the Appolonian and Dionysian of Spengler.

Not that there is really a clearcut division of types; not everybody belongs clearly to either of these two distinct kinds of people: just a relative predominance of the one or the other in many. But an egghead, by and large, is a person who has, as an intellectual, a predilection for, and a preoccupation with, abstract issues. The ability to form abstractions presupposes not only the basic intelligence necessary for syllogisms. To be able to see a common denominator between two events, one has to be able to establish some emotional perspective, some optimal distance in relation to people as well as to ideas. What is more, as soon as one is able to look at two forms of behavior or events and to see some similarity between them, one must have at least a measure of what psychologists have called "tolerance for ambiguity."

Some people need things always black and white. It is true that people of lesser intelligence can only work concretely. But some people with a technically very high I. Q. can see some important things only in black and white because it is emotionally impossible for them to stand ambiguity: black is black and white is white. They may have a hard time tolerating shadings because they need to think of good and bad in absolute terms. Only if the line of demarcation is very clear can they be sure of staying on the good side. Rigid walls are their solution to any conflict, any dilemma, in relation to people as well as to ideas.

It reminds one of the alcoholic who could stay sober only if he crossed the street to avoid passing a bar directly. If he walked close by, he had good reason to fear that he would stop in and get drunk. Most of us don't have to cross the street because the bar is not that much of a magnet to us. Literally, the frustrated old spinster may have to be particularly proper and on guard against all transgressions because her dammed-up libido has to be contained securely behind high walls, or else it might spill over. In distinction, the moderately normal married person is, in comparison to the adolescent or the spinster, ordinarily not too easily stirred by the daily sexual scene.

The eggheads are a constant threat to what I call, for want of a better term, the squareheads because they threaten the black and white and good/bad foundation on which alone the latter can find some peace.

Thanks to a number of social psychologists, one of the most outspoken forms of squarehead, the authoritarian personality, has been well described and can be clearly identified by test, etc. (the usual academic quibbling notwithstanding) as being precisely such a person with a low tolerance of ambiguity and a variety of definite developmental and psychological characteristics.

One social psychologist, Rokeach, has spoken of the open and the closed mind, characterized by an open and a closed "belief system." I would characterize eggheads then as having relatively open and squareheads relatively closed belief systems.

The "belief system" serves the squarehead as his guide to the world, close to "good" people and distant to "bad" people. Naturally "good" may mean different things in different subcultures: political, economic, racial, religious, occupational, and other values. From this system stems justification and rationalization for nearly everything one wants to believe or do. Since it is a self-contained system that feeds upon itself in a vicious cycle, nearly anything can be seen as support for the belief system, and anything

17

that is not so seen is perceived as wrong, dangerous, and to be destroyed.

Such belief systems were shared by the Nazis who were squareheads par excellence, shared by all varieties of religious and political bigots and race supremacists, who never hesitate to put to the sword, firing squad, or stake those who do not conform to their crazed notions. The missionary in Somerset Maugham's *Rain* is a good example.

Religious systems, organized religion, foster very firm belief systems. To the extent to which salvation is said to depend on certain types of values, prayers, behavior and customs, everyone not part of that belief system tends to be seen as alien, potentially dangerous and inimical. It does not make any difference whether that religious system is Catholicism, some variety of Protestantism, Judaism, Mohammedanism, or the animistic religion of some primitives. There may be a difference in zeal, especially in certain developmental phases when the urge to win over or kill the infidels may be stronger than usual. That such a belief system may bloodily divide people otherwise indistinguishable can for instance be seen in the bloody riots between Catholics and Protestants in Northern Ireland. These religious belief systems make it nearly impossible to live with the interdependence necessary in that community. It interferes with rational solutions of the porcupine dilemma.

As children are early imbued with religious belief systems and the price in some religions is very high (life and death, heaven and hell), these beliefs tend to be particularly strong and, by themselves, tend to make for squareheads—unfortunately, especially among the socially and educationally deprived .

Being members of one strong belief system—i.e., being some kind of a squarehead—seems to predispose one to susceptibility to other firm belief systems. The easy transition of Nazism to Communism and vice versa has often been observed. Similarly, religious squareheads are likely to be ethnic squareheads. Being steeped in religion as a hostile belief system makes one more vulnerable to having racial and other hostile belief systems. It is very doubtful that religiously intolerant people can be racially tolerant. What is more, riots in Detroit and Chicago support the notion that religious bigots are racial bigots and, politically, totalitarians.

Religious lobbies are strong and to talk at all critically of any aspect of religion is dangerous. Nevertheless, the ecumenical spirit will need further strengthening, bigotry further weakening, if nationalistic and racial strife is to be tempered. Children will have to be brought up without hate for people who differ in religion, as well as in color and language.

Obviously, to be a squarehead is a state of mind and, as such, ambiguous and worldwide. Some cultures, however, undoubtedly encourage the development of squareheads more than others. Germans have often been described even physically as squareheads, and certainly their whole character structure, with the ideas of precision, duty, patriarchism, is consistent with the characteristics of squareheadedness. Traits of Nazi ideology can exist anywhere, but it probably took a nation of "squareheads by tradition and culture" to give Nazism legality.

An egghead has an attitude of reasonable doubt, including self-doubt and, at least intermittently, an ability to see more than one side. A squarehead sees only one way, one side, and doubt is considered weakness.

Of course, some people may have only partially closed belief systems—that is, be predominantly squareheads only in one area of their functioning and not in others. A man might be a squarehead with regard to his business principles and quite an openminded person in relation to his family and social outlook. Mild forms of squareheadedness may not be more than what is generally called a "sober outlook": which often means keeping one objective in mind, to the practical disregard of alternatives. Executives, administrators are often useful and mild versions of this character structure; they are useful and even valuable if they do not get in the way of creativity.

Squareheads are necessary in many ways. Eggheads rarely become generals or even policemen—occupations which need not only prompt action on the basis of simplified or codified strong convictions (eggheads can do that), but also no self-questioning afterwards or the next time if one wants to retain peace of mind.

Squareheads are made, not born. Given a family, an ethnic, or religious group or subgroup, for whom repression plays a large role, most of the time squareheads will result if the repression begins early and is consistent. If a child is brought up restrictively, with strong punishment for any show of aggression, independence, or other drive, he most likely will become a squarehead. He will control his own quills so well that he will feel he has none—except some sanctioned by authority, in the service of authority,

or the "good" side. Being tightlipped and tight-sphinct-
ered otherwise, he will become the guardian of other people's good behavior to control his own. With face shut-
tered and eyes deadly dull, he has to deny any "bad"
behavior on his part and is often remarkably able to play
a double role hypocritically. He may sometimes in all
blindness perceive some evil in others where there is none
—see the mote in someone else's eye, but not the beam in
his own, the Bible has said. A psychologist has spoken of
this form of projection—of ascription of one's own inac-
ceptable drives to the outer world—as the "mote-beam
mechanism."

Of course, occasionally, repressive, punitive, rejecting
upbringing of a child is accompanied by all sorts of excesses
of drunken parents, hostility, too much close and intimate
living in cramped quarters, and sexual overstimulation.
Out of the misery of the child and the conflict of the tor-
tured human being growing up in this scene may come
some of the great creative contributions to mankind, artists, social reformers, great scientists. Greatness does not
have to be the result of such misery. That it is at times
is hardly compensation for all the harm squareheadedness
has done to human development all along. For the harm
to the thinker, burnt at the stake, for the many small and
innocent people who suffered from squareheadedness, it
is no brief for squareheads who have had a culturally re-
tarding, war-producing, narrow-minded effect, nor for the
zealot, of one kind or another, among the squareheads who
adversely affected humanity in all its history.

Humor is a characteristic of the egghead. It involves
the ability to laugh at oneself, at human foibles generally.

21

It also involves perspective, distance, tolerance of ambiguity, a measure of irreverence. The squareheads are usually sober men for whom the most difficult thing is to laugh at themselves every once in awhile—one of the most vital abilities.

Squareheads are often called realists. What this usually means, at best, is that they can see the immediate concrete reality. Often it means they are unable to see the reality around the corner because their vision is too narrowed by blinders. For that same reason, eggheads are often mistaken for dreamers because they are willing to forego some immediate goal for the sake of a larger though more distant one involving a good deal of "detour" thinking.

Squareheads are politicians. They are the people who always know which side their bread is buttered on, who plan details carefully and never take an unnecessary risk or even an unpremeditated step. Their emotions are controlled; they do the right thing at the right time for the right people. If this means making millions suffer or die, as it did in the case of the Nazis, it is enough justification that authoritative order made it right.

Squareheads and eggheads are breeds, however, which transcend national barriers, time, and culture. One of the most important, albeit invisible, battlelines crossing the earth is the one between eggheads and squareheads.

The small communities of the hinterlands, wherever they are, are prime spawning grounds for squareheads. Knowing only a restricted environment, having no chance to meet people who think differently, they face everyone else with the icy eyes and tight lips of their righteousness. The more isolated an area, the more squareheads per square acre. The insulated valleys of the Alps used to be excellent breeding places for squareheads. Each neighboring valley housed their deadly enemies of vast inferiority; a century after Napoleon's Waterloo, he still was their favorite enemy, rivaled only by Judas Iscariot whom they saw in everybody not to their liking. In some parts of Austria, where the percentage of Nazism was particularly high, the squareheaded population has managed for generations to be simultaneously bigoted, churchgoers, incestuous, patricidal, promiscuous, and feeling uniquely virtuous at the same time.

A squarehead should not be confounded with a fathead. The latter either is stupid or acts stupidly, sometimes goodnaturedly, sometimes out of petty greed and peevishness and small-time vengefulness. The fathead may appear to be a good fellow, even brag of his lack of intellectuality, seeing it as evidence of his earthiness. He has a dislike of the egghead because he cannot get over a feeling of unease that the egghead is smarter and might put something over on him. He simply does not feel comfortable with eggheads and willingly avoids them, if possible. Of course, he is delighted to give the egghead a little shove down a slide if it can be done with impunity at a good opportunity, and he feels reassured by the downfall of any egghead. Battling the egghead is, however, not his prime preoccupation.

For the squarehead, on the other hand, there is no greater concern, no greater enemy than the egghead. Understandably so, since the egghead's views could undermine the very foundations on which the squarehead maintains his vicious stalemate with himself. Let him get the merest shadow of a doubt that *his* earth is not the center of the universe, his way of life not the best, his religion not the most exalted, his conduct not the most correct, and the house of cards that is his life might collapse.

Therefore, one of the most important jobs for the squarehead is to watch the egghead and try to confine him and control him. Thus, intellectuality, the predilection for abstract issues seen with intellectual and emotional perspective, is always public enemy number one for "practical" politicians.

The trouble is, of course, that in our age of nuclear energy and constant sources of worldwide friction there is less and less margin for zealous error, for claiming the exclusive right to be right. The squareheads could drive our world into oblivion and not even have a chance for afterthoughts themselves.

Hopefully, it is possible that in our evershrinking world, with intense contacts of all people by communications media and travel, it may become increasingly more difficult to breed the creed of the squarehead. Also, increasing enlightenment in the upbringing of children would be excellent preventative medicine against the raising of little squareheads. For the little squareheads who can only think concretely in black and white because his toilet training was too early and too rigid may not only grow up to have an obsessive personality and maybe some obsession that could trouble him, he may well grow into an adult who finds an outlet for his obsessions which he considers rational—namely, that fluoridation or UNICEF or a mental health program is likely to undermine the moral fiber of the country. In that sense, personal psychopathology and sociological squareheadedness are only different facets of the same problem. Take the tragicomedy of a New York Ku Klux Klan organizer who also played an active role in anti-Semitism as well as other hate groups. When a reporter found out that he was not only of Jewish descent but had himself had a religious Jewish upbringing, he turned his ill-controlled hostility against himself and committed suicide. It is quite certain that a psychological study of other political extremists, especially their leaders and spokesmen, would also reveal a great deal of subjective disturbance.

Maybe some day children entering school will not only need a vaccination certificate but also one saying that they have been screened and found without gross psychological pathology (or are in treatment for their problems).

Major corporations not only have their staff psychologically screened but often conduct sensitivity training groups and other emotionally educative experiences. If some day all major public servants would be screened psychologically and have psychotherapeutic help for sorting out the emotional problems involved in their work, one might be more optimistic about our world.

4

Intelligence, Detour Behavior, and the Affairs of State

DO YOU KNOW in which way a ladybug and a lady are the same or alike? Well, they are both living organisms. While this common denominator may strike you as a bit low, if you can answer it at all you show the sort of abstract intelligence which intelligence tests examine in order to arrive at an I. Q.

To be sure, tests like the excellent Bellevue-Wechsler Intelligence Scale are carefully constructed, tapping many different aspects of intelligence, based on large sampling of the population and sophisticated statistics. The essential basis of such tests is still that a test result is pegged as indicative of normal intelligence if sixty-seven per cent of the population can properly answer it; that is the spread of the mean in a normal distribution curve. Sixteen and one-half per cent must fall above this level, and sixteen and one-half below it to qualify a test item as a useful criterion.

If you can stay with these statistics another moment, please keep in mind that these numbers add up to the fact that eighty-three and one-half per cent of the population have an average I. Q. or less (average is from 90 to 110). These statements won't mean much to anyone not accustomed to thinking in terms of test scores, but they are likely to make a pessimist out of one acquainted with testing.

And to be sure, in spite of recent outcries against excesses of test uses and overly rigid interpretations of I. Q.'s, a competently administered individual intelligence test is still a splendid instrument.

Let me put it in another way. About eight per cent of the population is composed of college graduates. For socio-economic and other reasons, a percentage of the population which would be intellectually capable of graduating from college does not get there. Nevertheless, roughly speaking, the college population corresponds to the intellectual élite. Any college professor is likely to tell you how depressing that thought can be, considering how little ability a good part of that college population has for abstract thinking.

And yet, the daily problems of our lives, our country, our world are becoming increasingly complex. They require not only increasing *knowledge* of any number of matters intricately related to the simplest problem facing anybody—such as fall out and milk consumption, DDT spraying and general health—but also the *ability* to utilize intelligently the information, in case one has it, and the

27

emotional ability to act on intelligently abstracted information, that is, the *emotional ability* to forgo the immediate gratification of one's needs for security, expression of anger, or of competitiveness, and to give up immediate and direct selfish desires for the sake of long-range survival.

"Detour Behavior" is a fancy term for an everyday phenomenon. A small child may try to reach for an object he can see through the cane back of a chair and get quite angry because he cannot reach the bottle he wants. Later, he will have learned that a small detour, a less direct way than the straight path, will get satisfaction which is sometimes barred directly.

Much of growing up is spent on learning to forgo some immediate gratification in order to get some or more of it in the long run. One learns not to polish off the jam jar a few minutes before dinner because this does not let one enjoy the steak at dinner.

One eventually does not always fight when one feels like it. One acquires a porcupine's hide and learns that the consequences of slugging it out when one wants to may be being hit by someone else, or punished by authority. One goes to school instead of playing ball, one goes through college instead of earning money immediately, one does not copulate behind the first convenient bush. In fact, one hardly ever has a chance to act directly on one's impulse. In that sense, detour behavior is a crucial mechanism in the rational solution of the porcupine dilemma.

Whether one likes this state of affairs or not, it is a fact of life, grown out of the necessity of civilized life, and is apparently on the increase. Thus, we now have more traffic regulations than in the horse and buggy days because the automobile moves faster, endangers more people.

Even nations have had to learn detour behavior. The UN is one of many attempts to delegate authority rather than act on one's own immediate impulse to mediate optimal distances. "To send the Marines" must have been a most satisfying impulse—for those who sent them—and very often the squareheads and the fatheads still want to send them. (The eggheads too, only they think it over before expressing this desire publicly.) Regrettably, if we send the Marines, somebody else is likely to send their men—and we might have a world war.

It is the burden of increased technical civilization, and maybe that of cultural changes, that it often becomes necessary for all of us, increasingly, to delay our first and second impulses in order to survive together. And it also becomes very difficult and more demanding intellectually to find another, not so obvious, solution.

In personal life, many people find themselves unable to have the necessary frustration tolerance to engage in detour behavior: the racketeer, the drug addict, the alcoholic, and the gambler share this characteristic need for gratification of impulse without delay. In fact, people as a group, as a lynch mob or as the electorate, have a tendency to want quick and direct solutions rather than complex ones—and thereby lies the problem of all honest and intelligent statesmen. In fact, it could be said that enlightened monarchs or benign dictators tend to enforce a certain frustration tolerance on part of the population, in its own interest. It is not a good process since dictatorships never stay benign, and the enforced frustration tolerance always leads to a variety of serious consequences: loss of a sense of responsibility and participation by the population, oppression of the masses by the few, and finally revolution.

Our problem is then quite clear: in order to comprehend the problems of our world, the many different aspects of one problem at the same time, to be able to see common denominators, to perform syllogisms, to draw conclusions from many different data, we need increasingly great intelligence.

To make matters worse, this ability, statistically demonstrated as a scarcity, needs to be alloyed with the emotional ability to postpone immediate gratification, to engage in detour behavior, for a greater benefit in the future.

One might find a source for pessimism in these reflections.

Let us take an everyday example to illustrate the last point. The matter of the urgency of foreign aid has made fair progress, but it is still by no means clearly seen as a vital matter of self aid, that unless certain countries are aided, their economy will fail, the market will be lost, and this loss, in turn, will affect the United States economy and political standing. The problem follows the ancient proverb of an ounce of prevention being worth a pound of cure. Everybody knows what problems of inertia this proverb tries to combat. The millions still uninoculated by Salk Vaccine, for instance, are evidence of the size of this problem. But, in addition, problems of modern economics, of global statesmanship, of technological advance are truly immense and complicatingly interrelated.

What chances are there that the roughly ninety per cent

of the population who are unable to state in which way a bee and a flower are alike (similar to one of the test questions of the Bellevue-Wechsler) would be able to (a) have the technical knowledge, or (b) the intelligence to arrive at the proper conclusions (particularly in the presence of camouflage by special interest groups), and (c) possess the emotional stability that supports intellectual findings necessary to respond constructively to issues of foreign policy?

The sad fact is that a large part of the ten per cent of the population who, by definition, in principle have the technical knowledge and the intelligence do not have the emotional qualifications. The special problem which we face in the second part of the twentieth century is that events move so fast. Until now, there was always enough of a margin for trial and error, for poor statesmanship, and immature behavior. The world has shrunk to where events in the Katanga Province of the Congo affect the man in Detroit as much as affairs in Rio, or Algiers, or Korea, or Moscow, Chicago, or Washington, or anywhere at all, and all of it at a rapid rate. This is not to mention the constant presence of the possible finality of a nuclear holocaust.

It is against the fact of human frailty, against a background of relentless technological advances that the corresponding political developments of dilemmas must be seen. There is a tremendous paradox in the fact that one needs a license to be a plumber and has to pass a Civil Service examination to be a file clerk, but it still takes no special qualifications to attain the highest political offices. What is more, high office has been attained in some parts of the country by singing fetchingly with a guitar and now by expert TV packaging. The fact is, of course, that an increasingly large amount of basic work related to legislature and the conduct of the affairs of state is done by expert personnel in the service of Congress or the President, and that, by and large, most of the lawmakers are often called upon to present their opinions on the basis of technical recommendations by the staff. One of their remaining tasks is to suit final decisions to the state of mind of the voters. If they are leaders, they use their own status for the increase of the emotional and intellectual tolerance of reality of their constituents.

The fact that there are some favorable developments is not a cause for complacency or disregard of the problems posed at the start of this contemplation: that in an increasingly technically complex society, an increasing number of decisions will have to be left to technically equipped personnel. This is regrettable because, in some ways, it certainly curtails an objective feeling of freedom of choice, if not necessarily the real degree of freedom. But the trend seems inevitable, however one may feel about it.

There is no question that a constant need for detour behavior can be very frustrating. At least occasionally it would be nice to be able to do what one *feels* like doing, rather than what one ought to be doing. That is where the dreams of being a beachcomber fulfill a function, as do the modern fairy tales that Hollywood produces, or the reading of mystery stories—irresponsibility in the one, glamour in the other, release of aggression via Mickey Spillane, and the reassurance at the end that justice triumphs. (Indeed, the popularity of the detective story may be based to a large extent on the fact that it is such a good antidote for the tolerance of delays and the postponement of our desires which reality demands. In the crime novel, the pace is swift and the anticipation of a prompt and satisfactory resolution at the end of the story is in pleasing contrast to the many uncertainties of daily living.)

However unpleasant detour behavior has to be in reality, in thinking of the alternative to frustration tolerance one is reminded of one of the great lines of Maurice Chevalier: old age is terrible, but the alternative unthinkable. If we do not choose reason, we face destruction.

Submission of the individual to society is the basis of society. In a way, the field of public health and education has led the modern trend. Once upon a time, matters of inoculation against smallpox, school attendance, social hygiene, and sanitation were personal matters and later political issues. Luckily, it takes no vote today to decide on proper sewage disposal or the management of certain epidemics. Public health personnel take care of it. The law enforcement practices are in a process of flux. The end may be in sight for haphazard, moralistic, and at the same time, cruel, handling of vital personal and social issues in the management of offenders.

Sooner or later, economics and "political issues" too will become divorced from power politics and efficiently handled for the benefit of all by technical experts appointed according to their competence.

That is not to say that the affairs of the world should be left to experts. As war is too important a matter to be left to generals, so the affairs of the Republic are too important to be solely left to the discretion of the experts. But the areas of expert management must increase, and the issues must be so narrowed down to generally understandable ideas that a population constantly striving to stay abreast of the times has a chance to make more rational choices than it has been able to make to date.

It must be obvious that in order for our civilization to survive it is essential that information and knowledge be widespread, and education in the broadest sense be considered crucial. It may well be that intelligence is not an absolute, finite quality, but may increase, even though it may do so within the pattern of the distribution curve. It may be quite possible that the overall capacity to comprehend complex issues may rise, as the presentation of these issues improves. At least, some experts on intelligence feel that it develops with increased opportunities.

It would be very good, indeed, if the moguls of mass media, like TV, would adopt this hopeful notion, and not always cater to the lowest common intellectual denominator.

It is equally clear that tolerance for ambiguity must increase, both by an intellectual process—as part of the education of children—and as a matter of emotional health.

Education of children in the public schools may play a most important role. Textbooks with perspective and teachers with open minds will help children weigh problems on the basis of reasonable evidence. Chauvinistic books and narrowminded teachers could be—in fact almost were—the death of civilization. Consider Adolf Hitler. Many things, undoubtedly, ailed him. His psychopathy, however, might well have taken a minor route, such as that of his half brother who served jail sentences for a variety of offenses, if it had not been for an obscure history professor in high school. This teacher conveyed square-headish, nationalistic ideas to Hitler as a panacea for his frustrations. Hitler remained grateful to this man his life long for the "inspiration" he provided.

Mental health, community mental health, and individual upbringing are becoming affairs of state. The personality problems which have driven ambitious men to hate and war and destruction start as "little" problems in the family, much as perversions, small scale criminality, and neuroses and psychoses do.

A striving for frustration tolerance and the emotional ability for detour behavior, the ability to settle for some warmth and not spear and be speared by crowding the other fellow are a matter of survival.

5

Personality and Character in Our Time

THE AGE of close relationships, of personal responsibility, and of compassion seems to be rapidly passing now, a victim of our modern technology. Only the youth revolt of the late sixties attempts to reverse the trend.

The outstanding feature of the last few decades has been a tremendous increase in mobility, socially, economically, geographically, and technologically. With the passing of the old order, the son of a village smith became one European dictator, while a paper hanger became his northern colleague. With the Second World War, the process was speeded up. Even the British class system crumbled, and prosperity brought more fluid society everywhere.

The airplane, rockets, satellites, and spaceships have shrunk the globe. The interdependence of the smallest area of the world with every other area is still daily astonishing most of us. Above all, the enormous impact of the media of communication makes for great psychological mobility because so much storms in upon us every day in so many ways and from so many sources that it is hard to involve one's emotions in any one problem. Because the world has shrunk to where everybody is everybody else's neighbor, and because of the effects of radio and television, we do not recover from Korea before Indochina becomes a crucial problem, then Formosa, Algeria, Suez, Berlin, the Congo, the Middle East, Vietnam, and a dozen other crises, not to mention A-Bombs, H-Bombs, Sputniks, Tel-Star, and fall-out for dessert. Once upon a time, the Dreyfus case or Sacco and Vanzetti could occupy the world's emotions for years. The equivalent today would be buried on page eight the second day.

The basic proposition is simple: every person has a fairly limited amount of energy, of emotional charge. It is difficult to be deeply in love with more than one person at a time. It is almost as difficult to be deeply involved with rather frequently changing acquaintances or places or events.

Yet, our modern world is one of fast change. People move a great deal geographically. The wars with concomitant personnel dislocations, industrial expansion, and particularly jet travel have increased mobility. This holds true not only for the wealthy but also for the skilled worker, the migratory worker in a trailer or a bus, the engineer who is shifted from one plant to another. At the same time, there is a great deal of socioeconomic change. Even if it does not involve a personal change in fortune, it means nevertheless that the total change of living standards and production makes many people live under vastly better circumstances than they were accustomed to.

Add to the economic and geographic changes the fact that communication media—papers, magazines, books, radio, and television—expose us to a much more heterogeneous scene than ever before. Because of all these means of rapid and constant contact with all the world, a newly-changing scene bombards us with every morning paper. Most of the time, we are served new crises with the breakfast cereal.

Given the fact that each of us has only so much emotional charge, and that there is so much to get charged up about, it is elementary that there cannot be enough emotion to go around to invest in everything happening around us. An increasing measure of non-involvement seems only a reasonable consequence. No wonder people do not get aroused enough even over vital issues, and that the "modern personality" seems a shallow one. It almost appears a necessary defense against becoming exhausted and overwhelmed not to become too involved. For our culture as a whole, the porcupine index may be on the increase. Understandably, the hippie answer is to do away with the cultural superstructure and increase compassion again. Society at large however reminds one of one of those apocryphal stories told about a Rothschild. The wealthy baron had been entrapped to listen to the hard-luck story of a pitiable fellow. Tears streamed down the millionaire's cheeks. Hope flickered in the eyes of the alms seeker when Rothschild stretched out his hand to ring for the butler. With a choked voice, Rothschild ordered, "Throw the bum out—he is breaking my heart!" Sometimes contemporary personalities seem constructed in a way to avoid constant heartbreak or becoming involved at all. Several shocking murders were witnessed by as many as forty people. They preferred to pull their shades or pretend not to hear to becoming involved.

Each historical era, of course, each culture, creates its own personality, and vice versa. Psychoanalysts wondered what happened to the florid cases of hysteria that were so frequently described by the great psychiatrists of the nineteenth century, Charcot, Janet, and even by Freud.

The fact seems to be that in the Victorian Era the gross need for repression of sexuality and other impulses led to such coarse symptom expressions as ladies' fainting spells, amnesia, paralyzed limbs, and the like. In our intricately fashioned mores, the personality and its disorders are more subtle, less obviously strange. Psychiatrists say that the psychoneuroses have been largely displaced by character disorders. The tightly corseted lady with smelling salts to her delicate nose has become the "Lady in the Dark," the woman executive, who finds it hard to play the feminine role. The convention-ridden and caste-conscious male has become the sophisticated but ill-at-ease organization man.

It is a truism that superficial features of mental disturbance change with cultural fluctuations. Schizophrenics who once felt plagued by the Devil now feel persecuted by electric machines or by radio waves. The first I knew about radar was when a Navy patient was brought to the hospital with delusions of being spied upon by radar.

The nuances of personality also change with the culture. The whole idea of humane feelings, of tendermindedness, is relatively new. After all, public hangings, floggings, and punitive amputations used to be general entertainment.

Once upon a time, one grew up in a community, took more or less an expected place in it. More and more, many families move, children grow up in different communities, move away from their families and friends, and often end in one or another large city, with relatively few ties to anybody. David Riesman spoke of the lonely crowd that is not tradition centered anymore or "inner-directed" towards its own ingrained values but rather anxiously adapting to an everchanging peer group. Erich Fromm before him spoke of the German people's escape from the uncertainties of unaccustomed freedom (attained by a loosening of socioeconomic barriers) into the serfdom of Nazism. The lessening ties of religion, the loss of the role of people like the family doctor, the impossibility of maintaining close friends, the weakening of marriage ties by more easily obtainable divorce, the relative strangeness of surroundings have made for more superficial relationships to most people around one. The principle is the same as we discussed before. The amount of available emotion simply has to be distributed over more people than ever.

Certain extreme manifestations of our society highlight these facts, bring them out in bold features. Social events like cocktail parties, or the mixed-up marital relations of Hollywood are especially blatant examples of a general situation.

With the anonymity that tends to engulf everybody, including the high school boy, comes a change in the feeling of relationship to the other person—the one one hardly knows. Because of the rapidity of occupational change so possible in our affluent society, the painter of today may have been a plumber yesterday and a salesman tomorrow. How can he possibly take his job seriously, invest the pride and personal satisfaction in it that he used to?

At the same time, not only the relationship to others is loosened, but even the one to oneself—to the various selves that we increasingly are in one lifetime. One's sense of identity is confused.

A story told by Billy Rose, the late successful Manhattan showman, is particularly illustrative of the lack of feeling of belonging in today's world of rapid economic change. He related that he often found himself almost tiptoeing into his sumptuous Westchester estate for fear the butler would throw him out! Part of him was still the poor lower East Side boy who had a hard time remembering that he was then the millionaire owner of the showplace.

The stories told of Skouras, of General Sarnoff of RCA, show their own attempts not to lose the continuity of their personality despite their own changes. Though the stories were probably fathered by publicity agents— the folklorists of our times—they have nevertheless the ring of truth when we hear the multimillionaire movie man talk about his days as a poor Greek busboy, or hear that Sarnoff still keeps up his efficiency on the telegraphic key in case he should become poor again and have to resort to his youthful means of livelihood. And former President Truman's court of cronies was probably another way of not getting lost in the sudden change into the most important person in the Western World. The role change brings a tremendous loss of perspective and identity, even for us smaller fry of lesser changes.

Youth especially grows up with very fluid values, swiftly altering with the craze of the day, the mood of the crises, the crowd in every new place they live. The friends of today are the strangers of tomorrow.

Under these circumstances, the degree of involvement with the next person, the depth of interaction decreases almost as a matter of personal defense. The deep emotions of past literary products, the romantic involvements of past dramas and even of movies are received impatiently or with derision. Techniques of stage and movie directors have changed progressively from rather stark emoting to the expression of feeling by indirection. Instead of a torrid love scene à la Valentino, the heroes of later movies are likely to make some flippant remarks which are followed by long shots of fireworks against the evening sky. The latest crop of movies and stage plays tends to have no action, no story, but rather impersonalized emotion. Emotions are permitted as "camp": a loveable absurdity.

Until the impact of the youth revolt, people's reactions were only skin deep. It reminded one of a phenomenon seen in recent survivors of concentration camps or other disasters. So much had been done to them that nothing could quite engage them emotionally again.

The constant bombardment of crises, the latent threat of nuclear war had a similar effect on all of us—after today, the deluge. Therefore, "let's twist": a dance requiring the partners to be several feet apart—little reaction and interaction—or the discothèque where frantic movement and stupefying noise take the place of human relationship.

Psychological and technological mobility make for fewer roots, more uniformity, in short, for the organization men. The tremendous impact of constant communication stimuli resulted in a numbed man of greatly decreased personal sensibility and responsibility, in a certain form of callousness, of impersonality. The youth revolt has reversed the trend.

Nevertheless, many facts of our lives had changed, apparently irreversibly, from the personal to the impersonal. Philanthropy used to be practiced by wealthy people, individually providing for the "deserving poor," or later through various forms of benevolent societies which dispensed aid in a very personal manner. Social agencies with trained professionals, rate schedules, and annual budgets, and social security provided by the central government have taken their place.

The family doctor who knew sometimes two or three generations has been replaced by a more scientific but often quite impersonal practice of a group of physicians or diagnostic centers. The chatty old grocery store has been replaced by the shiny, efficient supermarket.

In all these instances the problems of a growing fast-moving society with vast technological advances at its service have produced a change from the close personal contact (of less efficiency, higher cost, less choice) to remote impersonal service (of greater extent, speedier, and in some ways, better nature).

It would be wrong to say that contemporary man has no sense of responsibility; it is simply not a sense of *personal* responsibility, but increasingly one of institutional responsibility. It is not the attitude of the days of the robber barons, child labor, and debtors' prisons, but it is also not the period of individual social consciousness. It is the age of the welfare state, where one expects most problems to be taken care of, within limits, by constituted authorities and does not feel that they are, therefore, problems of one's own. Individual charity, like individual philanthropy, has been replaced by institutional provisions.

This state of affairs is by no means entirely to be deplored. Contemporary man, being the product of a predominantly urban, cosmopolitan society, is, literally, more urbane, albeit less personally so. Personality in the swift age of efficient technology may simply be adaptively one of smooth functioning and only transitory and briefly alighting on anybody or anything.

Until the hippies, love children, and student revolts, youth seemed transformed into a new type of personality. The surface was smoother in social relationships; involvement in people and ideas was less deep. Most important, these personality features did not cause any suffering; from being ego-alien, neurotic symptoms, they had changed into ego-acceptable character disorders, indeed just plain character structures. The rootlessness and lack of relationship were not perceived as unbearable any more. The lack of emotional commitment was not felt as deplorable emptiness, but as an admirable sense of realism and a capacity for organization.

The curious fact is that the super-organization man among the youth fitted smoothly into the impersonalized state, looking forward to pensions from college on, as Eisenhower remarked. These young people did not *feel* alienated, but they were so in fact from human values and emotions.

A turn of events came about with the enthusiasm of the Kennedy years. During the Johnson regime and in response to the Vietnam war, American youth became truly alienated and began to revolt.

Part of that revolt is that they discovered some identity for themselves, some emotional commitment as a group united by a lack of commitment to the values of the establishment.

Their personalities went through this change not only in America but apparently all over the world. The war in Vietnam stirred an international battle cry against establishments that have sent youth to its death in different wars. Above all, what they shared was a fear of atomic war. In our uncertain world, they decided, driven largely by fear and disenchantment with the world they found, to rediscover commitment, love, the simple values of life.

Only a relatively small percentage of youth is involved, but their sentiments have been contagious. Long hair is fancied even by truck drivers and staid businessmen, and pillars of the establishment have sat up and reexamined their premises.

Regrettably, a real change in contemporary society does not seem likely because the technological odds are against it. It is utterly unlikely that all the many developments of our modern civilization will be rolled back. It will be very difficult to remain a love child in a computer center. The best we can hope for is a slight influence of the youth revolt on contemporary society.

This may be particularly true because the undoubted

kindness and lack of viciousness among true hippies and other youth seem of a somewhat impersonal nature. Surely, they were exemplary of human behavior at the Woodstock Festival, but even their love of each other is one of live and let live, rather than one of deep involvement with each other.

If this assumption is correct, the youth revolt may hopefully have various good effects but is not likely to change the basic impersonalization of our organized society.

For that matter, the impersonalization need not be all bad, and in fact may parallel some of the sentiments of youth. Some of the admirable openmindedness of youth may be the result of certain features of our technological development.

If the trend of mechanization, impersonalization and their non-involvement continues, it is likely that intense group hatred, born of strong feelings of belonging to an in-group, as against an out-group, will disappear with the grouping. While people may more and more have only shallow and even transitory feelings of love and loyalty for each other, they are also likely to hate each other less intensively.

Individuals relate more urbanely than they used to. Take the case of the modern divorce, of the encounter of marital infidelity. The modern style is not to rise in wrath, but to agree more or less graciously to a reasonable settlement with a reasonable consideration for all concerned. Though this procedure bespeaks of less intensity of relationship (with Hollywood again the extreme, where children of different parents remarried several times are said to shuttle back and forth with the greatest of ease), it certainly is much to be preferred to mayhem and other tragedy. This trend toward courteous living in juxtaposition may even invade national and international relations.

If the North American continent leads in the dilution of interpersonal relationships because its socioeconomic climate permits the greater mobility and the high frequency of communication impact, Europe and other areas are following in the same path to the extent to which technology and affluence become their share. There are few familiar with the scene who are apt to doubt this trend.

It is very likely that the society of the future will be increasingly cosmopolitan, with looser boundaries, and urbanely uninvolved in the individual, though generally kinder.

In the society of our immediate future, it is very likely that Schopenhauer's porcupines will find their social needs regulated by a traffic policeman with a social science degree.

6

The Unsure Society

OUR SOCIETY is so unsure, alienated, uprooted because we have been exposed to very rapid change: of values, political structure, technical progress, including the field of military destructiveness, and economic facts.

With regard to the economic change, the unsure society resembles a nouveau riche—it has the affluence it is ill prepared for and suffers from the sudden change. The nouveau riche traditionally does not know about subtler values of the new sphere he has moved into, and he has left behind the values and morality of his past. He is on an uncharted sea, prone to be influenced by charlatans, ridiculous in his attempts to become cultured. He is like a person in a room with distorting mirrors because his values are as distorted as reflections in those mirrors.

A value feels like a value when one is accustomed to it, preferably from birth on. The division into lower, upper, and middle class—one's station in life—was something people were adapted to, and within their framework they had certain values. In fact, things, from shoes to houses, had certain stable values.

In our society of fast technological change, the values in one's life shift constantly, and that causes trouble even if these shifts are to the better. One feels alienated—that is, things feel alien to one because they are really not familiar as they vary constantly. What was unattainable yesterday is commonplace today.

Under the impact of mass media, changes in one place produce changes in another faraway place. Therefore the number of changes in any given place multiply, with changes in sexual mores, religious attitudes, nationalistic feelings, political beliefs. Ethical relativity means relative values, which, not being as firm as absolute, give one less of a frame of reference. This holds true in fashion (miniskirts), art (non-objective), even the role of age: what was middleaged is now young, what was immature at 14 is now grown up, what had status is now ridiculed, mistrusted, part of the generation gap.

Such a change in values was never quite as fast or as drastic, but a similar period of major change in the past produced similar social upheavals: the Fall of the Roman Empire, the ending of the Feudal Age, the age of machines, the end of the First World War and of the Second World War all brought a general restructuration of values. A minimum of safeguards, of workaday lines, is necessary to prevent chaos in a society which has more means for producing it in a major way than ever before in the history of the human race. An informed insistence on some basic values is necessary in sex, art, work, and all other spheres.

Money has a much less glamorous visibility than either art or sex, but the fluctuating status of money has a very profound effect on a society. If money maintains roughly the same purchasing power and if its supply remains stable, one has a conservative economy, and it is relatively easy to remain within a fixed framework of monetary behavior.

If the value of money fluctuates the psychological effects can be disastrous.

In our society, social progress has led to higher incomes for a vast majority of people. The various forms of social security, job abundance, and job protection have devalued money psychologically. The marked redistribution of wealth begun by the New Deal has blurred class distinctions.

One of the most blatant signs of the changed value of money is part of the generation gap: the toys children have now, their clothes, their general upbringing still keep the older generations aghast. The changing attitudes of high school graduates and college students towards jobs and job security are still a source of endless wonder to many who struggled through the Depression or the war years.

The quiet inflation, which puts the dollar now at about 50 per cent of its value of some 20 years ago, further adds to the confusion. A man who earns $25,000 now and still experiences it in terms of what it meant to him 20 years ago is at quite a loss because the purchasing power is only half that, not to mention the taxes which are hard to keep in mind.

Money is more fluid now than it used to be. Going

now and paying later is much more acceptable because there is more assurance that one will have money to pay later than there was 20 years ago. Keynesian deficit spending has become *the* mode of living, and many older people are still most uneasy about it and in conflict with the younger generation.

In fact, as the value of money changes from year to year, and advertising produces increasing appetites, and jet travel becomes more and more available, even the youngest person experiences value fluctuations which throw him off and make for unease. What was considered an exorbitant salary for a teacher last year is the routine today, and salary increases for policemen, firemen, and many others, especially in skilled, technical jobs, maintain a constant state of financial value flux in which the citizen feels strange and without a familiar frame of reference.

Surely there are many good aspects of the changes, including the upward movement of income. What causes difficulties is that a side product of fast changes in this sphere makes all frames of reference too fluid for most people.

With the rapid change in the financial stratification goes a change in social status, the role of work, and the concept of happiness itself.

It was iniquitous Feudal propaganda that the poor should know their place, and that knowing it makes one happy— be it black Uncle Tom or white laborer or craftsman. Not only in Feudal days, but also in pre-World War II Europe, status was very clearly indicated. Titles, not only aristocratic ones, but business titles (Kommerzialrat, etc.) were part of the landmarks. Similarly, in the United States, where one lived, where one shopped, the country club one belonged to, the bar one frequented were all part of the value system.

American society, however, has probably always suffered a little for the freedom of its ways. Unless one was a Cabot, a Biddle, or a Roosevelt, for example, a name meant nothing, except in small towns and in parts of the South. Intellectual position was worth little, be it as physician, or as teacher, or professor. It was all seen as "business." The ludicrous period of wealthy Americans marrying the titled of Europe was a special form of attempting to attain status in a more or less status-free society.

Status has now become even less stable because of the socioeconomic mobility of our society and the general quick tempo. Those who attain signal successes are soon crowded out by brand new celebrities and forgotten.

For some, affluence has become a goal in itself. For others, complete repudiation of the establishment values has become a kind of anti-goal. In either case, there is now less pride than ever in a job well done. In part this development is a result of socioeconomic changes. The value of competence, though internal, had its external roots in the fact that such a reputation was vital for one's support, for job security. In a society of abundance and fast mobility, such a value is neither necessary nor very well possible, since hardly anybody remains well known long enough to attain benefits from a good reputation.

The trouble is that we seem to be the kind of animal who can have inner self esteem and happiness only from the relatively stable values, from doing work for the work's sake, *ars gratia artis*, and as soon as all success is only a means to an end (of money, etc.) rather than somewhat of an end in itself (the satisfaction of doing something right), some inner dissatisfaction results. The "outer directedness" Riesman has spoken of is largely a result of the increasing lack of inner values and is an attempt to make up for lack of internal structure and guidelines.

Happiness in the sense of stable inner values may escape the affluent society unless some vigorous effort is made to provide values.

If the unsure, affluent society is indeed like a nouveau riche, some of the factors which sometimes help those newly rich may also come to the rescue of our society.

Part of the remedy for nouveaux riches lies in the passage of time. They themselves may become a little more accustomed to their new value system—but above all the next generation behaves differently. Their second generation often rebels in their adolescence and at the same time —and certainly later in their life—are usually very comfortable in the world into which their parents brought them and in which the parents themselves could not feel quite at home.

The hippies are to a certain extent the second generation of our affluent, unsure society. Their parents do not really know what to do with the new affluence and technological advances. The currently young generation is truly born to a plenitude of jobs, as well as to the atomic bomb. Like the sons of old revolutionaries, of small shopkeepers, and union leaders, they accept the new luxuries with boredom. Many adolescent children of the newly wealthy are sarcastic about their parents' Cadillacs, clothes, and status-hungry friends, while moving with none of the selfconsciousness of their parents through the country clubs and luxurious surroundings. Their parents are still on their best behavior when they enter the hotel in which they maintain a luxury suite, but the adolescent offspring feels at home in it in dirty dungarees or formal dress.

The second generation of moneyed people sometimes shows flaws. They do not want to work like their fathers, but they do not have the internalized values of Rockefellers. They therefore sometimes become wastrels, playboys, or other kinds of misfits. It often takes the third generation to have become accustomed to the affluence, to have developed inner values that make it possible for them to work hard and be useful, while taking some privileges and comforts for granted enough to enjoy them sensibly and constructively. They are able to make choices in the values they want. They may forgo flashy cars for a valuable stamp collection, may forgo all sorts of ostentation for a comfortable home.

If our unsure society is a society of nouveaux riches, it may be possible that mere getting accustomed to the new world will produce a generation that will be more ready to settle down to internalized values because it did not find satisfaction in the excesses brought on by sudden freedom from want, economical and sexual, and the freedom to move in all directions.

The hippies try to return to some internalized values— of love, self sustenance in the communes, basic teachings. Squareheads attempt to return to the safe values of their childhood in defiance of reality. Hippies, at the same time, still rebel too much because they are also overwhelmed. The next generation, or the generation of hippies in their later lives, may be able to choose values they want to accept and others they want to reject.

My favorite criterion for mental health is the ability to make a choice—to be sociable one time and isolated another, to be industrious sometimes, and lazy or relaxed another, to be free and unfettered sometimes and highly disciplined another. In more obvious forms of impaired mental health, the neurotic has to avoid heights, crowded rooms, or open spaces; in less obvious forms, his life is limited by emotional stereotypes, determined by childhood distortions of the perception of people and the world.

The best criterion for social health may also be a society which is *able to make choices of its social values*, much as laws must be developed in response to the needs of each development in society. Legal regulations are developed where social problems arise. Traffic laws arose with the automobile and the airplane, and will sooner or later develop for outer space.

Social values, like legal regulations, are in essence an ecological problem of man's interaction with his environment. Overpopulation and pollution are the result of technical developments—of greater hygiene, lesser infant mortality, antibiotic drugs which keep people alive longer. Pollution is the result of more cars, more factories, the development of plastics and detergents.

Regulation by law of any of these activities, including the having of children, is as inevitable as it is likely not to suffice. Just as a wealthy man may decide not to use all his assets, our wealthy society may have to decide not to employ all of its chances for development until society is ripe for it.

The space race may be a good example of this problem. We are moving into space because we have the technical knowledge. We may not really be prepared to use space advantageously, but to use it rather for military control of earth, for competing with the Russian Joneses, and other primitive needs. It might well be an example where both the Russians and we might have to agree, like corporation executives in an exclusive country club, not to cut each other's throat by trying to outdo each other. Unlike nouveaux riches anxious to have more and more shiny hardware, it might behoove us to choose to cultivate our dirty backyard full of unsolved social problems.

Solving the social problems of the unsure society is urgent for reasons other than the inherent problems themselves. An unsure society is a frightened society. Like a frightened person, a fearful society is an irrational society, likely to engage in all the destructive ways of unreasonableness: war, social suppression, above all, regression in all forms of living.

The vaunted idea of the silent majority becomes a haunting one if one thinks of it as the unsure majority. Such an unsure society can survive only with optimal leadership. Such a leadership must incorporate, have internalized itself, the highest values of civilization in order not to lead society down the path of self-destruction.

The dangers are great. The more unsure someone is, the easier it is to think in black and white terms, to be more of a squarehead. At sea in an evershifting value system, the tendency is to oversimplify the concept of law and order. The tendency arises to deify order of established, or once established, values because they are some straws to hold on to.

In that sense it is easy to lead the silent, unsure, frightened majority. One can get them to remain silent, or even to become noisy and enthusiastic about their being led to perdition. Hitler's Germany is not the only country that could shout itself hoarse with enthusiasm about being led to ruin. It has happened before and can happen again.

We have to move between the Scylla of lack of any rules and the Charybdis of rigid retrogressive rules. To be either anarchic in the rejection of all values or cling destructively to childishly oversimplified and outdated values is easy.

It is difficult, but important, to retain perspective without losing a frame of reference. Intellectualism is important: to see all sides of an issue and then choose, rather than seeing only one side or seeing all sides only to be paralyzed by inaction.

In the long run, the fate of our society lies in education—an education for an ambiguity of tolerance and with enough information to make possible intelligent choices based on many perceived possibilities.

In the short run, our fate is determined by our political organization, by the guarding of the freedom of expression, by vigorous critique of the powers that be. If our society is lulled into being a silent one, the majority interests will be sacrificed to the shortrange interests of the ruling few. The shortrange interests of the ruling few are shortsighted not only for others but for themselves. Eventually, such defect of vision and interest has always led to destruction of these very interests. Therefore, it can truly be said that guidelines with a stable perspective for all and for the long run are in the interests of everyone, even those who most fight against them.

7

In Broad Perspective

WHILE THERE HAS BEEN an increase in the frequency of human contact since the beginning of the century, the intensity and overall quality of it has decreased.

Along with this increase in *quantity* goes a change in *quality*. The intensity of the individual human contact has decreased since the beginning of the century, more so in the last decade. Intensity is in part related to duration: the more mobility, the more fleeting the contact. We pass each other not only geographically by all available means, but changes of all kinds are frequent: jobs, mores, art forms, socioeconomic changes of all sorts. Whatever the nature of the news item, it disappears faster from public interest than it used to. In general, we know more people and about more things—and less of each of them than ever before.

The hippie movement and its parallel developments are attempts to deal with this limited intensity of human interaction. "Love" is in part meant to be an answer to the impersonalization of a technical civilization. Whether it really accomplishes any deepening, even for the few directly involved, is questionable. At times it seems that all they manage is to live more amiably *next* to each other, rather than *with* each other. Drug-induced "trips" are certainly an isolated event for the individual, rather than a form of human interaction.

Some forms of contact—other than the direct personal ones—have gained in intensity. Try to escape a saturation advertising campaign or a political one! It assails your ears from loudspeakers, radios, TV. It attacks your eyes in leaflets, bus and subway advertisements, sky writing, and even subliminally.

A large personality factor enters into the Porcupine Index (P.I.) in several ways. In the first place, a stimulus has different emotional values for different people. For example, an Irishman is more likely to feel human impact from an item about fighting in Belfast between Protestants and Catholics than from one about fighting in Libya. In the second place, people differ with regard to their sensitivity to any impact or human contact. One could call it the "princess on the pea" factor. There are those who get headaches from noise and become nauseous from too much light, and there are others who turn up the hi-fi to maximum and feel best in a room where there is standing room only.

It pays to speak of an overall P.I. that would include all input, human as well as inanimate. And in distinction, we would set up an S. P. I. or Social Porcupine Index which would deal only with human contacts.

The S. P. I. can be much more intricately developed.

Human relations are not only characterized by plain *number* of people one is in contact with, but also by the depth of the relationship and the quality of that relationship. If everybody has, arbitrarily speaking, 100,000 Freudian units, we have to ask how many he keeps self-centeredly invested in himself, and how much on Annie, and how many on John. The more he invests, the deeper the relationship.

Some people *have* to have close relationships. Others can sometimes be alone and at other occasions choose close relations. A third person needs to be always at a distance from others. *To be able to have a choice,* to change one's pattern, is probably the most adaptive, the healthiest way of being. Therefore, flexibility in one's social relationships deserves another separate rating.

In this way, the pattern of the P. I. is a qualitative expression of one's personal social adaptation in a contemporary world which threatens to overwhelm us with maximal quill input, as stated by the numerical value of the P. I.

There are many personal ways and many attempts on the part of society to deal with social impact of all kinds. Individual defenses make for fascinating and sometimes bizarre personalities.

The social defenses include legal provisions for the restriction of the noise level, for traffic signals, and sometimes futile attempts to turn back the clock. Often the multiplying regulations meant to hinder the pain of interaction become a prime source of discomfort themselves, and unrest results.

Periodic spurts of scientific and technical progress throughout history have produced new forms, often violent, of human interaction. The invention of gunpowder as well as the development of machines in general and of the printing press in particular produced powerful changes which no amount of machine storming or scholastic proscriptions could control. Most interestingly, Jean Jacques Rousseau won a competition of the Academy of Dijon in 1749 on the theme: Has the progress of the sciences and arts contributed to the corruption or the improvement of human conduct? His reply is well known, and our current period in history seems to be full of counterparts. Instead of his belief in the Noble Savage, we have encounter groups. The idea seems to be that if one only returns to the simple life and directness of human contact (preferably via the skin, in California), all the sting can be taken out of human interaction.

Much of our current social and cultural revolution is a necessary and understandable reaction to overkill and overcontrol by state and science. Youth has a right and a reason for being dissatisfied with the world they came into, and to be scared. Surely we are handing them an affluent society, but we are also handing them an unsure society: a society the survival of which is threatened by atomic weapons; a society in which values change so rapidly, morally, economically, politically, artistically, that youth feels a lack of identity. These unstable values are in some ways more easily borne by middleaged people who may be bewildered but not totally imbalanced, because they still have a commitment and a value system which they acquired in their youth in a time of relatively less rapid change. In that sense, youngsters born since Hiroshima are probably more realistically oriented with their fears and rebellion than those in their forties and above who simply cannot quite comprehend the world we live in, however inappropriately. However, much of the reaction to the dire state of our world is silly oversimplification, an exaggerated swing into the opposite reaction. Savages were not noble, and feeling one another's bodies lovingly is only a very partial solution of a limited problem. The idiocies of collages of flotsam or black dots in a frame are no more an artistic answer to dealing with emotional human needs than the tasteless sexual gropings in movies and stage productions. They are attempts to find the right distance, to find warmth in directness, but they are excessively reactive to the evils they mean to counteract, anti-rationalistic and not constructive enough.

To make love instead of war seems a fine idea, but is not an answer to all problems, at least not for us more limited older people. To use drugs when relating becomes too painful will not improve the human interaction.

Unhappily for man and luckily for porcupines, Schopenhauer was a better philosopher than a naturalist. Porcupines can lay down their quills, but people hardly ever can, if at all. All we can do is study the nature of the human animal and attempt to find the best possible means of getting along with each other. These means must allow a great deal of fluctuation, backing and filling, in individual transactions as well as in national ones. Built into the system of facilitating relatively painless interaction must be flexible boundaries for variable adaptation. For square-heads, there are only black and white answers. Eggheads can tolerate a measure of emotional ambiguities.

Education, including the affective upbringing of children, will have to be the answer to the future of our world. We must bring up children who can have flexible values without discarding a value system per se. Values may be relative, full of snares and delusions—but some delusions are vital for survival. A system of values may be axiomatic —that is, arbitrary and, by itself, unprovable, but it is necessary. The simplest formulation of such an axiomatic value system might be to find those rules of personal, national, and international conduct which permit the optimum of individual happiness with a minimum of painful interaction. It would have to be part of that axiom that the propositions derived from it must change with changes in the world's living condition.

The study of the best solution to intercurrent changes in world conditions must be a constant concern of social science in the broadest sense: jurisprudence, sociology, psychology, and economics, among others. Maybe it would be clearer if we would call them *survival sciences*.

They are the sciences we especially need to develop to help us survive the progress other sciences, notably physics, have made.

Not that there is reason to feel hopeless—only desperate. For reason has marched along, albeit straggling, way back at the rear of technical progress. Unlike more primitive societies, we usually delegate personal grievances to the police and the courts. Unlike only a few decades ago, labor and management hire arbitrators rather than goons. Unlike periods of starvation and hapless cycles of depression and inflation, we have controlled economies and social security. Rousseau also became aware that return to nature was no real answer. Our social controls, the League of

Nations and the United Nations, correspond to the basic ideas of his *contrat social.*

All the "social contracts" are steps of progress, steps in the direction of easing the problems of living together. True, some of the corrective measures themselves produce discomfort, even illness: as the tonsils are lymphatic tissues guarding against the progress of germs into the interior of the body, at times becoming inflamed or primary foci of disease needing treatment, our social guards occasionally have similar fates. Most of the time, however, they perform their tasks efficiently and quietly.

True, also, the curve of progress has many dips, but the trend is unmistakably upward. In many ways, American society, with all its evils and pitfalls, demonstrates this best. It takes visits to underprivileged countries, to much of Europe, to understand and appreciate the advances contained in American society.

The dignity of man is very much a function of his social security and the amount of redress insured by his society. In most South American countries and in much of Europe the *official* is still the lord of the manor and the servant of the powerful few. The daily attitude of the average citizen to his policeman, postman, and tax collector mirrors the true amount of dignity he possesses. Without a free press as a source of redress, without the ordinary democratic process predicated upon relative financial security of the individual, there is no individual dignity.

There has been an upturn in Europe since the Second World War. Even before the Nazi catastrophe, there had been fraternization among the young of many countries. War was anathema for many, and class structure had become less rigid. In social democratic Vienna, people wore informal clothes, drank more milk than wine, and greeted each other with "friendship." Not so bad, even if the slogan was not "love."

The Nazi period was a horrible dip in the history of mankind, almost certainly its most dangerous. Despite that crisis, one can say that a certain amount of progress has been made. I do not agree with the cynics who say that today's love children are the Madison Avenue executives of tomorrow. The current generation of adolescent children is not the same as their parents were. At 45, today's parents are much younger than *their* parents at that age—healthier, more flexible, better informed, having more longevity before them. Sexual mores were more reasonable when they were young than in their parents' time, long before the current topless revolution. A good deal of what the current adult population fought for, against their elders, has become accepted reality.

There is no time for complacency, but also none for hopelessness. Our youth has grown up into a world radically different from the one of the previous generation. Youth is meeting its world with some reasonable adaptive measures and with some confused, anti-rational, overreactive, childish ones. The role of intelligent, enlightened adults is to help them secure reasonable changes and protect them against the waste and the dangers of nonsense—dangerous because *all excess invites excess*. The Nazi episode was largely possible because there was a lack of structure in German post-World War I society. An excessive lack of structure today could invite similar dire developments as a "backlash."

IN BROAD PERSPECTIVE

There is danger, also, because we are in a race against time, more intense than humanity has ever seen. Our technical progress may not only kill us by overpollution, overpopulation, and overexposure to everything; it simply demands more intelligent thinking than is currently available. The amount of intellectual and emotional detouring necessary for modern man to adapt himself to the world he has made is tremendous. Surely, even the available intelligence of traffic sign makers has not been able to keep up with the increase in speed and numbers of automobiles.

II. In a More Personal Key

8

History Is Our Destiny

THE TYPE of individual relationships one has with people in adult life is largely determined by earliest relations in childhood. Systematic observation of infants and some experimental work with monkeys suggest that infants need social contact as if it were nutriment. Even if they are well taken care of hygienically and nutritionally, the absence of warm human contact will lead to depression, apathy, withdrawal, even physical illness and possibly death. A certain amount of sensory input in infancy is essential for the growth of the organism. Experimental neurological work suggests that afferent nerves carrying to the brain impressions of the world around us stimulate growth and development.

Carefully controlled work has shown that infants with

too little human contact have a lower body temperature than those with appropriate interaction! Movies of infants and their mothers illustrate that tense attitudes on mother's part can produce an overactive child. In turn, little maternal contact may produce children with little need for, or ability to utilize, human warmth.

Our history is our destiny. To understand the person sitting opposite you, you have to know his past; or at least it is often the easiest way, and sometimes the only way, to understand the presence of anybody or anything.

When electric shock treatment was still much in vogue, it was necessary to keep track of the time the convulsions lasted. Annoyingly, the wristwatches used stopped working within a few weeks. In no instance could the watchmaker find the fault. As the same thing happened to several psychiatrists, the cause was finally inferred. During the treatment, one would be in some bodily contact with the patient, and the "spill current" occasionally caused a burn under a ring. That same current apparently magnetized the watchworks. Knowing this shared history of the watches was the only way of understanding their behavior.

Geologists, as many other scientists, also make some of their best inferences and predictions (e.g., where to find oil) from knowing the history of a particular piece of the earth's crust.

Dynamic psychologists may seem to disagree a good deal. Most of the arguments however involve only the fine points: *what* particular personal characteristic is due to *what* historical cause. In several research projects it was possible to use the ordinary methods of science—understanding, prediction, and control—to test some hypotheses.

Psychoanalytic sessions were recorded with the patients' permission, and three analysts were asked to serve as independent predictors and judges. Starting from the taped session material, they judged what was going on and predicted what would be going on next time, on the basis of clearly stated propositions. Years later the experiment was repeated with brief psychotherapy. The results showed respectable ability of several psychoanalysts to agree on what was going on in the patient and, to a certain extent, to predict how he would behave in future sessions.

While the correlations were good, they were not perfect. Of course, few if any scientific data are perfect. There may be other reasons, however, why psychological theories based primarily on personal history may not be perfectly explanatory of current behavior, porcupine index, or anything else.

Some children, for instance, may be born with more of a need for human (and other) interaction than others. One has to think of some children as having a pronounced *stimulus hunger*: almost from birth on they are especially interested in what goes on around them. They respond to everything more intensely than the average child. Clinical impression suggests that such children often grow up into people who need a great deal of human contact, lively colors, loud music. If they can't have these stimulations, they feel depressed, empty. And if they feel unhappy, extra stimulation is their attempt to cure it. Stuffing themselves with food is another form of stimulation for them, and it's hard for them to understand why they tend to overeat. One should hasten to add that such a congenital predisposition for stimulus hunger may not lead to trouble

73

at all if early infancy is need satisfying. Only if maternal deprivation coincides with such an Anlage is a real emotional problem likely; here, as in many instances, individual experience and genetic history interact and modify each other.

In the last decade, reinstating the role of innate factors in personality growth has reduced the burden of parental responsibility. It would be a mistake, however, to underestimate the importance of the human environment in childhood for later social relations.

For a long time after all, mother, or her substitute, and the other close figures, constitute the whole world for the child. If that world is friendly, warm, and giving, that is how the child and later adult will tend to perceive the rest of the world. If that cosmos is ungiving, rigid, cruel, or remote, that is how the infant will grow up to know the world. One's perception may actually create the reality.

In an oversimplified and selective way, it is useful to say that the child starts having all sorts of perceptions from the moment he is born. The adult we meet can then be compared to a complex composite of perceptions, not unlike a composite photograph of innumerable components. His contemporary perceptions are structured by past perceptions, sometimes excessively so. A certain past image of father or mother may unduly color one's perception of, and reaction to, authority figures, as if one were seeing the person through special kaleidoscopic eyeglasses.

A person may be as unaware or unconscious of the influence of some of these past perceptions as one is usually unaware of the components of a composite photograph, or the subtle influence of advertising on making choices. Much of unconsciousness is unawareness of the effect of past perceptions on our current perceptions.

One takes on the characteristics of the people close to one, for better and for worse. What they say and do becomes part of one. *What was external perception becomes internal structure* of the personality. To choose something very trivial: three generations of one family all had a tendency to shake a door three times after they locked it to make sure it was really locked, and without being aware of the fact that they had "learned" it from each other! Usually, of course, much subtler and more important things are "learned." By identification with the significant figures around him, the child acquires values, moral structure, and, above all, forms of relating to others.

This fact takes on much more concrete meaning if you meet a patient in a hospital who hears voices accusing or admonishing him. Often, these voices can be very simply identified as those of a parent. Indeed, some of the more unfortunate nagging, demanding, blaming, became only too well internalized, so much so that part of the personality could not coexist in any kind of peace with the rest of it and was disowned, split off again by the patient. Now it seems to him that not his excessively vicious conscience is speaking to him, but some real person. As the delusional and hallucinatory experiences are a jumble of past experiences, he is not able to untangle them and reintegrate them with less conflict. Therapy can sometimes help do that.

Psychoanalytic treatment takes so long that some claim calluses from the couch. The reason for the long duration lies in the fact that analyst and patient together have to try to understand the contemporary distortions in terms of the past distortions. By sampling the daily thoughts and feelings and notions, they find common denominators between current misperceptions and past experiences. When the patient sees and feels the common denominator between some current irrationality and its historical source, he has something like an "aha" experience. As in all learning, some of it is spontaneous, like a click, seeing how it hangs together. One click, however, is never enough in learning arithmetic, or golf, or to drive a car. It then takes application of the newly-learned perception, over and over again, to a variety of situations. In analysis, this process is called "working through" the acquired insight in daily life situations. A third way of laborious learning takes place in relation to the analyst. One is likely to feel towards one's doctor the same or similar suspicious, overly dependent, or fearful attitudes that one has experienced with parents and others in the past, and in relation to all sorts of people in one's daily life. In what is called the transference relationship, one has a laboratory situation for studying one's forms of social relationship and learning about one's peculiarities.

What is unique about the psychoanalytic process is that it is able by subtle unlearning, learning, and relearning to undo a great deal of the effects of the past on the present behavior of a person. The breadth of the character and personality change possible is unique for the psychoanalytic process. That is also why it takes so long. Without such change, however, many life histories develop with the tragic inevitability of the classical Greek drama.

Some Other Personal Distance Regulators

There are children and adults who have a great deal of stimulus hunger and can never get enough of social contact. There are others who hardly interact at all. Little reaches them, and they respond minimally to any stimulus. In the extreme, we call them *autistic*. Some may start out that way by biological Anlage; others may get that way because of their early history: they were shown little interest, little friendliness, and did not learn warm interaction.

People vary with regard to their *stimulus barrier*. Some have a very low one and everything affects them; they react to everything and reach out for more. That is true especially for people with a manic makeup. Others, who also register everything, try to get away from social and physical stimuli because they are unpleasant for them. This holds true more for the depressive makeup. Some people shift from elated to depressed phases, and they seek or avoid social contact, noise, and lights according to the phase they are in. The more or less healthy person scans stimuli, selects people and situations to react to, and is inattentive to others. The autistic people may have a particularly high stimulus barrier. Little reaches them, and they react to less.

Field dependence and field independence are other characteristics that influence one's social climate.

Experiments have shown that some people are dependent upon their surroundings for most of their cues. Some people cannot tell whether a window frame is upright or not if they do not have the usual setting in which to see it—that is, with other upright objects. Other people can tell whether the window frame is upright without any other cues because they get their main orientation from their own body. These latter are field independent, the others, field dependent. The fact is that field dependence or independence involves much more than such simple perceptual problems. Socially, innerdirectedness and outerdirectedness can be closely related to field dependence: needing other people to set standards. If one takes one's emotional cues excessively from others, such as being affected by the ugly mood of a lynching crowd, it has been spoken of as "emotional contagion." Suggestibility is related to it. It is obvious that some people would have to seek close social relations simply because they need other people to tell them what is right and what is not. Their field dependence makes them look for closeness and their Porcupine Index appears high, but hardly because they are healthy extroverts. Politically, their lack of identity and independence makes them followers, for better or, in the long run, for worse.

If this need for closeness is very marked, child psychiatry has spoken of *symbiotic relations*, taking the term from general biology. Symbiosis means living together, two organisms joining forces for mutual support. Some infants may start out with that need, others get that way because their mothers have a need to live symbiotically with them. They tend to the child's needs the way they want their own needs taken care of. They may dress, drill, and educate the child for their own satisfaction. The child may well grow up having only the one goal of, in turn, satisfying mother by his achievements and internal behavior. Such people, when grown up, are likely to seek

78

to find symbiosis again in friendship, in marriage, and in work. Politically, they are what a dictatorial regime lives on.

Purely psychiatrically speaking, if someone grows up symbiotically, he will suffer from problems of identity. Because his life was so closely intertwined with his mother's, he hardly knows where his self ends and his mother's begins. In fact, this may be almost literally so in people who have such an extreme disturbance of their body image that one could say they do not know where their body ends and the rest of the world begins. A very uncomfortable symptom that results from it and may be serious when extreme is called "depersonalization." One feels as if one were not real, or as if part of oneself were not real. It is a feeling not identical with but related to a feeling of the world not being real. Of course, almost everybody has a little bit of that feeling occasionally, as a déjà vu in a strange city, or after some very upsetting experience.

Problems of identity are of much concern currently and the favorite topic of existentialists. In a narrow sense it means that some people need friends, lovers, accustomed environment, (have, in short, a very high P. I.) because their sense of identity is otherwise severely disturbed. In a broader sense, our current youth revolt is in part due to a lack of identity in our insecure world. They find some comfort in close living and a joint front against the establishment.

Luckily, some children grow up in a relatively benign, constructive atmosphere which permits them to develop an identity. Treated affectionately, they adopt that attitude towards themselves and others. They are, to a certain extent, sufficient unto themselves and do not need others constantly for orientation, approval, or regulation of self esteem, but relate flexibly to them.

People who are field dependent, stimulus hungry, symbiotic, or have identity problems are at the mercy of the temperature of their human environment. They are even excessively affected by the physical environment: chances are that depressed people, those unhappy with themselves, not only need human warmth, but also respond much more markedly to warm weather and sunshine than do others.

Much of life consists of attempts to regulate the warmth of the human environment, to live according to one's own porcupine index, within different settings. We need people who can adapt flexibly to our quickly changing world.

Man's Inhumanity to Man Is His Revenge for the Indignities of Childhood

Neurosis and psychosis, delusions and hallucinations are not the only results of a painful childhood. Neurotic and psychotic behavior results from taking the conflict out on oneself, changing one's own personality. There are people who combine that process with also taking it out on others. Whether in neurotic or psychotic proportions, or as psychopaths, they are rigid, cruel, selfish, even bestial and fiendish because they were treated that way. Only organic brain lesions of one kind or another allow some exceptions to that rule. Otherwise, one only needs the reservation that seemingly relatively subtle inhumanity to a child may result in grosser inhumanity to others by that adult person.

If a child grew up in a consistently emotionally cold home, it is likely to become a detached mother, a reserved superior officer. The Porcupine Index will be a safe indicator of the past, and vice versa (the oversimplification is slightly guarded against in the word "consistently"; in homes where the emotional attitudes vary from time to time and from person to person, the outcome is much more complex).

The Beast of Belsen and similar creatures, wherever they are, are in part determined by their "opportunities." Thus, the social setting or the legal situation may determine how much of their cruelty is expressed manifestly and in what ways. The main cause lies in their childhood. The historical factors may not have been parents who behaved like concentration camp guards, but parents who were brutal in their disregard of the child, overstimulating sexually, unfeeling in ordinary situations. The German character may have lent itself more to Nazi mentality and concentration camp practice than other nationalities to the extent to which German parental behavior was more rigid, brutal, and cold than that of parents of other nations. As unfortunately all peoples have some parents who treat their children inhumanely, all nations are likely to produce some bestial specimens. While relatively normal people attempt to reestablish something like the warm climate of their childhood in relation to their friends, the misfits create in adulthood the only environment *they* knew in childhood: all vicious quills and no warmth, the werewolves of legend.

Thus, the relations of porcupines and men are formed early, for better and for worse. While most of us give and seek warmth, man's inhumanity to man, be it of smaller or greater dimension, needs little philosophizing. It is his revenge for the indignities of his childhood.

Some Social Aspects

While some individual foundations for the personality are laid as described, other factors determine one's relationship to others. The cultural matrix—mores and taboos —and value systems are of immense importance in shaping personality.

In our current society, value systems are less stable than they used to be. Human contacts vary more because children and their parents have more geographic mobility, while television broadens their horizons.

Individual as well as cultural factors need to be taken into consideration when we are concerned with the effect of childhood development on our future society.

Our complexly interacting society needs especially well-adapted people to deal with the burdens of our civilization. One needs to be better able than ever to forgo immediate personal gratification to adapt to the needs of all the other people with whom one is interdependent. There is less room for chauvinism, for rigid opinions, because the world is more and more one community.

The means for control and destruction are greater than in past times. Not only atomic weapons but also the communications media can be misused by a political variety of Big Brother. Paranoid extremists of all kinds are more dangerous to society than ever.

If personality and adaptive potential are largely a result of upbringing (few if any would doubt that upbringing at least determines the development of liabilities and assets if it is not their actual cause), then it follows that attention to the upbringing of children assumes greater social importance.

The responsibility of society for the individual has steadily intensified with the degree of interaction. In the area of child care, compulsory schooling, compulsory vaccinations, and other measures have long been with us. Very reluctantly, American society has come to grips with its responsibility for some of the crudest forms of parental behavior towards children. The battered child syndrome has finally alarmed enough people to have brought about social machinery and legislation to deal with the thousands of parents who beat their children to death. (The reluctance was great to interpose society between child and mistreating parent.)

Yet there is little doubt that society will also have to assume responsibility for the emotional upbringing of children if we are to avoid dire sociopolitical consequences. No doubt there is reason for valid concern about further invasion of civil liberty. Certainly, the absolute minimum enforcement should be exercised, and maximum stress placed on education.

Everybody who can spare a sperm and an ovum can be a parent, but only few are well equipped for it. For some reason, no training has ever been considered necessary for this most difficult of all jobs.

This training is important but still not an answer to all problems. Some parents are themselves too disturbed to bring up normal children and will have to be singled out for treatment. Some children are so disturbed because

83

of their upbringing or biological nature that they need treatment, among other things, so as not to become social dangers and misfits like the mass murderers and political lunatics.

Without legally enforceable treatment of emotional and behavioral problems, we will not make enough of an inroad soon enough. Contrary to popular opinion, there is enough agreement among all the diverse schools of thought to agree that a constantly abused child of alcoholic or deranged or otherwise severely disturbed parents is not likely to grow up healthy. A jury of sociologists, jurists, psychologists, psychiatrists, and social workers could judge individual cases and all possible safeguards must be employed, to avoid bureaucratic arbitrariness. Essentially, though, the step is unavoidable.

If we can insist that a child be vaccinated, a food handler certified to be without contagious diseases, an automobile driver able to see, there is no reason why society should not insist that parents be able to bring up children healthily rather than endanger society with them.

If man's inhumanity to man is the result of the indignities and mistreatment of his own childhood, it is high time that we take the necessary steps to protect humanity by protecting every child's growth and development.

9

People Pollution and Mental Disease

"Population increase can be reduced to zero only by laws which make sterilization compulsory. Such laws will be passed only when a significant majority in a given nation are ready to accept them. Biologists may propose such action now without committing professional suicide; politicians cannot.

"I propose that: 1) Voluntary sterilization be encouraged and all costs involved therein be paid by the government. 2) Sterilization of any female who has produced three offspring be made mandatory by law."

From a letter to the Editor of Science,
January 23, 1970, Vol. 167, pp. 334-335*

"A big change is taking place in the language of politics. Officials are not only talking about home affairs rather than foreign affairs these days and tossing around a new vocabulary of environment, pollution and ecology, but they are talking about 'control of the growth of population.'

---

* Copyright © 1970 by the American Association for the Advancement of Science.

THE PORCUPINE DILEMMA

"They are saying, in short, that the United States will not be able to 'control' pollution of the atmosphere, or the rivers and the seas unless it 'controls' the population of the United States, and this word 'control' is being used quite consciously now as a substitute for 'family planning.'"

James Reston, New York Times, January 21, 1970*

SATELLITE COMMUNICATION, jet travel, and technological progress in general have closed the gap that long served as a buffer between different countries and different cultures and peoples of the world. The decrease in spatial and psychological distances has inevitably greatly increased the amount of interaction among us all. Consequently, we are witnessing the impact of new sorts of contacts and impingements among diverse populations, sub-groups, and individuals.

Imagine the possible and probable effects of the new complexity. Mutual and automatic respect for each other's rights came easily when encroachment upon territorial rights posed no threats. Before the world became one economic community, there was no need to suffer the consequences of stringent import-export regulations. However, it is harder to find the optimal, geographical, and interpersonal distance for psychological and physical needs in today's overpopulated world of complicated communication networks. When people lived in rural areas rather than in crowded metropolitan centers, delinquency, vaccination, pollution control, birth control, and sewage disposal worried almost none, nor was there much reason for the aver-

---

age person to care. Disease then had less opportunity to spread. Destructive emotional attitudes were more encapsulated and less likely to contaminate. Now, with the closing of the buffer gap, disease-carrying insects in one tourist plane flown from Asia or Africa can threaten us with an epidemic here. Events in Mississippi have repercussions in Nairobi, and tin production in Bolivia can affect industry in Detroit.

An especially cogent issue is a long string of regulatory practices initiated by the Federal Government which makes almost everybody unhappy, at one time or another, be they people on the political right, left, or center. A clear trend of increasing control and regulation during the last few decades over what any individual in whatever sphere is able to do can be documented almost ad infinitum. For example, the gigantic steel industry has been forced to control its prices lest uncontrolled spiralling affect the total economy adversely. Today, controls over the sale of firearms, governmental reactions to practices in the pharmaceutical industry, influence on the medical profession directly or indirectly by Medicare, a wealth of legislated employment practices, the furor and then the actions taken to ensure mandatory safety devices in automobiles are but a few of the thousands of examples illustrating the direction in which we are headed.

In the field of medicine, especially in the public health sphere, there is of course a long list of regulatory practices, most of which we are so well accustomed to that we neither question nor even notice them any more. There are laws concerning food handling, sewage disposal, compulsory vaccination, as well as treatment and, if necessary, confinement of any and all suffering from serious contagious diseases. Only when some new and controversial general health measure is proposed do we find marked public sentiment, such as in the case of fluoridation of water. While one must expect some publicly expressed emotional turmoil as a legitimate response to potent controversial issues, we seem nonetheless committed to the view that law takes precedence over "laissez-faire" in certain circumscribed areas within the province of the public health aspects of medicine.

Psychiatry increasingly has entered the fields of public health and preventive medicine in recent years through the vehicle of community psychiatry. Indeed, the community at large experiences ample need for psychiatry to enter this broader area of health concern. It still holds true that, on any given day, half the hospital beds of the nation are filled by psychiatric patients, and half of those, or one quarter of the total, by schizophrenics. Studies of metropolitan populations, as well as those of rural areas, suggest that around 80 per cent of the population may be more or less severely affected by emotional problems. The subjective suffering produced by emotional problems is matched by the burden of a tremendous financial cost, 20 billion dollars a year, seen both in maintenance and custodial care of the mentally ill, as well as in the resulting lost manpower, diminished creativity, and generally lessened productivity. Moreover, our increasingly technological society will become less able to accommodate mental disturbance.

The point is that primary prevention of the more virulent emotional difficulties may be the only answer to these problems, and the only effective way of getting enough primary prevention may be by stating the scope and limits of legislation for compulsory psychiatric treatment, and then enforcing that legislation.*

In recognition of the preventive and public health role which psychiatry is to take, the Federal Government proposes to support as community mental health centers those necessary but not sufficient facilities which will provide the customary inpatient facilities, outpatient departments, day hospitals, and research capabilities. The Government also insists that 24-hour clinics be made available like the Trouble Shooting Clinic I originated in 1958.

I had called it the Trouble Shooting Clinic at the time to emphasize that it was not, strictly speaking, a psychiatric clinic dealing only with established (in the sense of overtly entrenched and discernible) emotional problems, but would be dedicated as much to "primary prevention" as to "secondary" and "tertiary prevention." In keeping with the sense that the public health people are accustomed to using these designations, in speaking of primary prevention we refer to dealing with situations and problems before they attain pathological status. In secondary prevention, we want to deal with the acute problems before they become worse or become chronic; and in tertiary prevention, we are concerned with rehabilitating those who have

---

* My ideas concerning the need for legal safeguards of emotional health comparable to other measures in public health were developed several years ago. As any legislation depends as much on the spirit (with which it is implemented) as the letter, I feel that the current climate of general restrictions of civil rights is not a good one for implementing my recommendations. In principle, however, I consider my suggestions as necessary and appropriate as restrictive covenants concerning pollution control or compulsory vaccination.

become chronically disturbed with respect to their optimal functioning level.

My own earliest experience in this area involved attempts at primary, secondary, and tertiary prevention with patients suffering from tubercular and cardiac illnesses—specifically to help them avoid a psychological invalidism secondary to their somatic problems. I was again impressed with the importance of this kind of work when I placed a mental health team into a medical-surgical emergency clinic for a year with the hope of not only detecting patients with definite emotional problems, but also of helping to engage in primary prevention of emotional difficulties in patients as well as their families. The patients involved were afflicted not only by emotional disorders, but might also have been traffic victims, and others customarily showing up at an emergency clinic. It is not difficult to imagine how crucial to a family's viability adequate help would be in avoiding socioemotional disorganization when the breadwinner has secondary psychological invalidism along with his accident.

It is one thing to offer help, even around the clock, and another to have people accept it. It is by now quite widely agreed that people coming to mental health services, even suicide prevention centers, are not necessarily the ones who most need the help. Conversely, people who need it most both subjectively and objectively from the standpoint of their effect on others around them are the last people to know it or to seek help.

Generally, in the field of public health we have any number of laws which either help find dangerous disease carriers or force them to undergo treatment if necessary.

These laws are applied when education and information have failed in the particular instance. As mental health has definitely become a branch of public health, it seems only reasonable that a similar supplementation of the educative process be a legislative one to deal with our epidemic proportions of emotional disturbance.

For legislation to be of value, it is first necessary to know the conditions to which it might be most effectively applied: the areas where we have well-documented knowledge (whether from formal studies or direct observation) of the circumstances under which a given emotional difficulty will occur. It is also, of course, necessary to predict this occurrence with a high degree of accuracy.

An illustrative study was reported by Josephine Hilgard and M. Newmann, who investigated the circumstances of onset of psychiatric illness in a state hospital population. They found that among a significant percentage of patients, women especially, onset of illness occurred exactly when their oldest child was the same age as they had been themselves when they lost their own mothers. What we know of this type of "anniversary psychosis" suggests that the mothers might have identified with their own children at that significant age, or that other factors then produced a powerful enough echo of their own traumatic episode to make them ill. Using one's imagination in looking ahead, one wonders how it would be if computers could give us the date, for instance, on which women living in a given community might be approaching that dangerous point specified above. We might then offer them group therapy as a prophylactic measure, dealing with this specific problem with the hope of decreasing the incidence of actual

91

illness. Let us assume that Hilgard and Newmann's findings would be firmly substantiated by other investigators, and let us assume that we demonstrate that indeed some such group therapy could more than halve the incidence of this type of psychiatric disorder, what questions would be posed as to the community's obligation if it turned out that 95 per cent of all those so afflicted did not care to enter therapy?

Another case in point: many of us have encountered children, or for that matter, adults, who in their childhood were seriously affected by some badly thought-out divorce arrangement. Very often, divorce arrangements acceptable to the parents involved are simply agreed upon by the court. Needless to say, the divorce settlement concerning the children is often arrived at on the basis of irrational emotions of anger and vengeance, with little awareness or knowledge of the needs of the children. For instance, mothers are almost routinely given the custody of a small child, yet little is being done to provide or see that there is an adequate male identification figure in the child's life. Often the father's visitation rights are little more than a farce. It would seem reasonable to expect that the court, aided by mental health experts, might be more actively involved in assuring the optimal psychological arrangements in an effort to minimize the possibility that children of divorced parents would sooner or later suffer from divorce-related psychopathology.

Of course, such a proposal brings us to a sensitive area, involving the broad issues of civil liberties and human rights. What if the parents, divorced or not divorced, should not be agreeable to any such court-suggested arrangements that would be intended to safeguard the psychological health of their children and, by implication, the future of their community? Does the community have a legal, moral, or other right to enter in and enforce the issue? On the face of it, it would appear that if the community has the right to insist that children go to school, be vaccinated before they enter school, that children with contagious diseases may not attend school and may have to be in isolation at home, then it also might have the right to insist upon certain aspects of ensuring the mental health of a child. If the community has the right to protect itself against sick food handlers, should it not also have the right to protect itself against emotionally ill parents and children?

The point could be made that the protection of the many against the few is as necessary in the field of emotional disorders as in the field of physical illness. The Typhoid Marys carrying real bacilli around with them are no more dangerous than the emotional Typhoid Marys who carry danger of contagion of emotional illness among everybody they contact. A few especially dramatic examples are available. For instance, Lee Harvey Oswald, suffering as far as anyone could determine from an emotional disturbance which, according to reports, carried him politically from the extreme left to the extreme right, and then to nowhere, was able to kill the President of the United States. Where could there be a more striking or painful example of worldwide repercussions due to the act of one disturbed person? Oswald was presumably correctly diagnosed by qualified personnel in the mental health field when he was a child, but there were no legal provisions to enforce treatment when his mother withdrew him from it.

The Oswald case, the murders of Robert Kennedy and Martin Luther King, the recurring cases of mass shootings and killings by disturbed individuals and thousands of other crimes suggest that the upbringing of children may have to be more of a community concern than it has been in the past. Even some very obvious aspects of child-rearing have so far been barely dealt with from a total community perspective. The battered child syndrome underscores the responsibility of physicians and the community to protect children from physical violence and also help those parents who cannot control their own violence to avoid bringing about the disasters so familiar to all emergency room personnel. A project in Denver offers the opportunity for parents who experience on-the-spot violent impulses toward their children to call a psychiatric service day or night for immediate contact, advice, and aid. (It appears that the problem most often causing undue parental violence is children's continued crying.) The *Journal of the American Medical Association* reported that child-beating may account for more deaths among the very young than automobile accidents; and yet, without specific legal sanctions, few people, including physicians, assume the responsibility of reporting such instances. If the rearing of children has remained such a private concern that there is hesitancy to step in when a child is being beaten to death, we can imagine what resistance there might be to the idea that extremes of psychological mismanagement of children by their parents should be interfered with by law. Yet the psychologically-damaged child of today may not only be the burden of the local community tomorrow, but also a definite threat to it, and by extension, to the world community as a delinquent, as a rabblerouser, a demagogue, a private avenger, an assassin, or a mastermind of genocide. He may in fact be the one who presses the button that could destroy us all.

In considering legal measures to help eradicate inequities in the mental health fields, a number of methodological, medicolegal, and ethical questions arise in conjunction with the complex context in which they occur. The first and most obvious question is whether we know enough about the specific causes of emotional disturbance in children and adults to know unequivocally, or even with reasonably high probability, how to prevent them. A corollary question is whether there is enough agreement within the diverse elements of the mental health profession itself, considering that the lay public hears a great deal about divergence among different schools of thought. The fact is that mental health professionals, like those in any other science, do not know enough to always speak in absolute certainties. Viewing emotional problems along lines analogous to the medical model of illness, we might well be reminded that in medicine generally, and in public health particularly, measures often have had to be taken on relatively insufficient information and improvements postponed until all the etiological factors were completely understood. Sulfa drugs and penicillin saved many thousands of lives before there was any clearcut idea of the process by which they managed to kill infectious bacteria. If we should want to wait until the relationship between illnesses and their treatment is completely understood, we should by all accounts still not be taking aspirin for even a simple headache.

Divergence of opinion among the experts does exist. Nevertheless, there is probably a large area of very basic assumptions upon which all schools of thought in the mental health profession agree. I do not know of any school of thought which would claim that cruel treatment, lack of understanding, social isolation, and exposure to family strife are beneficial for children. It may indeed be true that some survive as relatively healthy even under extremely adverse conditions, but then it also holds true that some people may be exposed to plague or tuberculosis and not contract them. That is little reason for not protecting the general population against exposure to the plague or tuberculosis. We do know something of the ways childhood trauma affect adult functioning, so the proverbial "child is father of the man" is indeed well founded.

There is, however, no doubt that we know too little about certain specific aspects of the problems of prevention, diagnosis, and treatment of certain mental disorders, some of which have especially important consequences for the community. For instance, the problem of acting out—that is, of committing destructive asocial and antisocial acts—is so far not diagnosed to any satisfactory degree even by the most skillful mental health experts. Again and again, patients are being released from hospitals who in due course commit rape, murder, and other mayhem. Statistically, it is probably true that the crime rate of people identified as psychotics is not greater than that of the general population. Even so, the nature, bizarreness, and context of the crimes committed by those who are grossly mentally ill call dramatic attention to themselves.

There is also no doubt that many aspects of present emotional problems are not primarily, or certainly not exclusively, of psychiatric or psychological concern. Today, as ever, sociological, socioeconomic, and other factors are also influential. No amount of psychiatric help will prevent or treat problems deriving from incredibly crowded living conditions, from racial discrimination, and from economic deprivation. Many problems terminating as psychiatric ones may need non-psychiatric prevention.

It is equally certain that whatever societal body might eventually make decisions concerning necessary preventive measures to ensure optimal emotional health, (e.g., a jury system of experts), that group should include sociologists, social workers, jurists, and others, aside from psychiatrists and psychologists.

Before one even contemplates the technicalities involved in promoting effective prevention, I think it is legitimate to ask again and again whether legal measures enforcing prevention are indeed necessary. Certainly, educational measures should be maximally employed for the same end. Some years ago I thought about starting a "School for Parents," consisting of small groups of not more than a dozen parents having children in certain age ranges to discuss typical problems. I saw such group sessions as having a two-fold function: first, to simply provide information—a mixture of Gesell, Freud, and Spock; and second, to function to some extent as group psychotherapy where emotional problems could be dealt with in this mode. At the same time, if some parents would appear to have more than ordinary problems, they could be singled out for individual attention.

There is also little doubt that some existing legislation is not being maximally used these days. With the threat of expulsion from school, school principals could exercise a great deal more control than is currently customary. Because of personnel shortages, we are not even using other professionals optimally in connection with courts and other public facilities. Undoubtedly, the problem of personnel will be raised in discussing the possibility of legally enforced preventive care. While this problem exists, increasingly better technical handling of these problems should make the same number of professionals considerably more efficient.

One might suspect that even with the full use of the educational approach and better utilization of existing legislation, there may still be a relatively small area in which further legislation will be necessary for the protection of the interests of the community. As it happens, New York State has already initiated one fairly controversial piece of legislation: that of enforced treatment of drug addicts. It seems only a small step from there to broader legislation of this nature.

To be sure, one cannot take seriously enough the danger to civil liberties and individual freedom which might result from any legislation that would make it possible for the local, state, or Federal government to step in and tell a parent that he is not fit to bring up a child, and that the child needs placement, or that the child needs treatment whether the parent likes it or not, or, for that matter, that the parent must undergo treatment whether he or she or both of them like it or not. As a matter of fact, in addition to raising problems of individual rights and liberties, the prospect of government regulation raises new technical problems for the professions concerned, since we will undoubtedly need to know more about the psychology and treatment of people who do not volunteer for treatment, especially by psychotherapy. The problem is not entirely new or unsolved, however, as it is reminiscent of the more familiar situation of successfully treating people whose disorders are quite acceptable to them, or, technically speaking, "ego-syntonic." Nevertheless, a great deal more needs to be known for mental health workers to be able to carry on such treatment effectively—even if mandatory therapy should appear desirable and legally justifiable and required. The dangers of imposing current fads in educational thinking and in psychiatric thinking must be fully considered. Big Brother in the form of a psychiatrist or the mental health profession is not more attractive than Big Brother in the form of big government or undue coercion of any other kind. But mental health, even as the result of legislated measures, makes possible the most important of all freedoms: freedom of choice of behavior, unfettered by neurotic limitations.

In sum, considering the trend of increasing interaction in all spheres of life coexisting with increasing legislation, I believe that the likelihood and need for such legislation enforcing psychiatric treatment by law in certain instances is very great. However, the situation is still beset by enough problems and enough dangers that we can and should at the very least arrange for panels of experts consisting of lawyers, judges, psychologists, social workers, psychiatrists, sociologists, and anthropologists to consider the matter carefully from all sides. Whether one likes the prospect of legally protected and enforced mental health or not, I believe the time has come at least to start the dialogue. Primary prevention may never be successful enough without the effective backing of relevant further legislation.

10

Cold-Blooded Animals, Warm-Blooded Animals, and Identity

"COLD-BLOODED ANIMALS" is a popular misnomer for some creatures, for instance, the reptiles, who tend to adapt their body temperatures to that of the environment. Thus, the blood of a rattler lazing in the sun is a lot hotter than that of his brother in a shady glen.

Humans, on the other hand, are different from snakes in that respect. To call them warm-blooded is to misname them equally grievously, however. They are what the scientists call homoiotherm. They have a good built-in thermostat which keeps the body temperature pretty evenly around 98.6, if all is well.

The same can by no means be said for the emotional or social equilibrium of man. I don't mean that one might get hot under the collar or frigid, as the case may be. What I mean is that for some people it is a lot easier to maintain their emotional equilibrium, their feeling of well being, than for others. It almost seems as if some people's sense of adequacy, of being loved and esteemed, fluctuates with the environment they are in. Only if surrounded by companions who clearly express their warm sentiments for them, or only in the presence of symbols of approbation, from medals to flunkies, to good cloth to adoring members of the opposite sex, do they seem to feel well. If faced with even temporary lack of such sustenance, their self-esteem drops to levels below tolerance, and they will do anything to prime their system.

Everyone knows manifestations of this lack of a built-in love and esteem regulator. In an innocent form, there is the gregarious fellow who is depressed if alone. Noise and crowds are his life stream. Riesman's "otherdirectedness" is also a form of this disorder. As far as this phenomenon can involve social or political behavior, it may constitute a crisis of conscience. To conform to society is "normal" by definition—that is, a form of normality can be defined as behavior consistent with 67 per cent of the population. On the other hand, conformance with a disordered society, such as the Nazi-gangster covenant, or a lynch mob, must be considered failure of a personal internalized indicator of what is right and what is wrong. Without a commitment to the absolute standards of a Kant, it is not too difficult to establish a range of norms which seem to have transcended history and cultures.

Some lucky people seem to be the other extreme—they have an unshakable thermostat, and they are able to maintain their "self" almost unaffected by events. Franklin Delano Roosevelt may be an outstanding example, if his biographers report correctly. He seemed to listen to everybody, pass from task to task, and somehow always remain the same—albeit not in very openminded communication with anyone. In fact, it is questionable whether FDR was not already a little over the line of ideal self-regulation of sameness, of maintaining one's identity and sense of oneness. Many of his close collaborators report that they could never be sure of what he really felt or thought. As great a man as he was, he may have been a forerunner of the basically uncommitted, however intellectually committed he was to maintaining right and decency and freedom.

The curious and alarming fact is that the sense of self, identity, and equilibrium can be overdone, beyond the normal. Maybe that is not so different from the body's reactions, after all. If the blood temperature can't rise to the occasion of warding off a streptococcus invasion, things are pretty serious. And maybe if one remains entirely unperturbed in one's sense of self, things are equally serious. The borderline between normality and what psychoanalysts call a narcissistic character can be very thin in such a case. Does one remain unperturbed and strictly one's own self because one has an appropriately stable built-in system, or is it because one has such a self-serving, insulated system that the external events fail to register properly?

That is a question which is raised in respect to people of extremes, from Lenin to de Gaulle. It often seems as if reality would register only minimally on such people, sometimes to their detriment, and sometimes to the ill luck of the world.

The psychiatrist's office, of course, is filled primarily with people whose own emotional temperature is excessively dependent upon external events. Middle age may be such a precarious time because the devices which help maintain a feeling of self-esteem and external identity tend to fail for one reason or another. The beautiful female finds decreasing reassurance in the mirror or the salon. The intelligent male may have had comfort from grades, fellowships, degrees, and other kudos. Increasing income and status tend towards diminishing emotional returns. They cannot continue to accrue or they lose their meaning, as the next likely achievement is to be the most successful person in the cemetery.

One of the many nearly impossible tasks in the upbringing of children, then, is to raise them with an optimum of an internal stabilizer of self-esteem, of selfness, and identity: to give them values of others and themselves which keep them this side of self-righteousness and yet not leaves tossed in the storms of life.

As with much of the upbringing of children, this goal is not easily attained. The child has reason to feel overwhelmed by the big, unintelligible world around it. It takes loving care to reassure the child and give it a sound feeling of security and being loved. The moment an invisible line is overstepped and a child is too well protected and too much loved, it will fail to have a firm feeling of identity and self-assurance. For if a child does not get a chance to battle some odds and find itself successful, it cannot develop self-reliance and self-sufficiency any more than the child who is constantly overwhelmed by terror, lack of love and of approval. As with vaccinations, a child needs just enough of a challenge to strengthen itself by the development of antibodies and not so much of a virus that it succumbs.

Childhood experience becomes the structure of the personality. It seems to be part of normal childhood experience to be loved and found worthwhile. Such experiences seem to equip a person with a permanent sense of being somebody in his own right, and external events do not shake him unduly in the future. If, on the other hand, this normal process of being esteemed does not become part of one's system, one may try most of one's adult life to attain that feeling of worthwhileness, and usually not quite successfully. Much as the feeling of being held dear is as necessary as physical warmth, one could modify Descartes for some people: *I am loved, therefore I am.* If not at least appreciated, they may even feel physically cold, unreal, and have to move close to somebody, simply for survival. Sometimes, of course, stuffing oneself with food or drink, feeding oneself or being a bottle baby may be a substitute.

If one grows up without a sturdy thermostat for self-esteem, for maintaining the internal self-esteem, one may have to employ all sorts of means for regulating it by external measures. It may well be that addictive drugs often serve that purpose. More certain it is that all of us employ various means to maintain our identity within a group, to obtain or retain the esteem of the peers, and by that token our own. That process holds as true for the drug addict who may sometimes "mainline" to show that he is not a sissy as for the businessman who contributes a little more than he really feels like at the fund-raising dinner, for much the same reason. However, the particular need of being accepted by one's peers may never be higher than among adolescents. As they revolt against the establishment of their elders, identity within, and approbation by, the group are absolutely essential for them. This explains the extremes of clannishness among adolescents, be it in a street gang, among rightwingers or leftwingers, fraternities and sororities or a motorcycle club.

In the sense of having a firm identity and not being excessively dependent for one's emotional tone on the external approbation, only a reasonably well-adjusted person is likely to be a nonconformist in a wholesome way: that is, able to be a nonconformist as well as being able to conform.

For to be a constant nonconformist in a relatively healthy society can certainly be one of the many forms of trying to regulate one's self-esteem in a more than ordinarily disturbed way. Lindner has popularized the dramatic form of the Rebel without a Cause. In this case to rebel has become a style of life. All of behavior seems to hinge on an imaginary goal, a fictitious goal (as Alfred Adler called it, who also coined the term "style of life" in a technical sense) to pay the world back for some infantile wrong, poorly understood and badly overgeneralized.

Acting out impulses based on fictional unconscious goals is by no means limited to rebellious psychopaths or other wayout personalities. Such behavior may be only occasional and obviously impulsive, or may be based on an intricate character structure which pervades an entire life.

Take a very bombastic businessman who engages in an imaginative sales campaign. He is full of enthusiasm, driven by the greatest urgency. He feels this campaign will add a great deal of scope and income to his already successful company. He spurs on all and sundry. His associates, however, answer with relatively limited enthusiasm because they have already been through many such campaign ideas of his. Some succeed admirably, and others fall flat. The organizer, however, behaves like a man possessed at each campaign. He seems to have no meaningful memory of previous and similar inspirational episodes, and he is sure that this is the best of his ideas and will indeed make *the* difference.

The fact is, however, that he loses most of his zest well before completion of the campaign. This takes place whether it is successful or not because compared to his fantasy expectations, no campaign can be good enough. And before too long he is off on another idea, while his associates suffer from fatigue from the last one.

In a minor key, the sort of person just described is common enough so that nearly everybody knows someone similar. In extremes, this sort of behavior is found in people suffering from manic-depressive psychosis. It is an old clinical truism that if one scratches a manic, one finds a depressive. There is the old story of the man who sought help from a doctor for his extreme unhappiness. The doctor of the old school pointed at a huge advertisement on a billboard across the street proclaiming the wonders of a leading clown in the visiting circus. When he suggested that seeing the clown would make the depressed patient happy, the poor patient replied: "But I am that clown!"

Be it professional funnyman or patient, the excessively happy, the manic is trying desperately to salvage something of his self-esteem by ignoring, denying, avoiding some unpalatable fact. He feels totally unloved and clowns around to make people laugh, love him, applaud him. Manics may either engage in fantastic business deals and other ventures to salvage their feeling low and out in the cold, or they may simply make up stories. I recall a patient who impartially either actually bought warehouses full of things he did not need and could not afford, or simply told everybody that he had. That way he felt big and appreciated by the people he bought from or those he impressed. On the other hand, a very good salesman is often a person whose self-esteem may be increased by being able to make the other person buy something. *Emptor caveat.* Such a salesman will feel all the more aggrandized the less desirable the merchandise was or the less the customer really needed it. One wholesale merchant I know of would at times leave his administrative offices to sell some small item on the floor, preferably off the back shelves, to boost his mood and self-esteem. In that case the sale had the meaning of besting the other person. It was simply a device for regulating his low self-esteem. For others, medals, titles, clothes or deference by the headwaiter may serve for everyday needs of supply of esteem.

This feeling of attaining the upper hand may be part, though not all, of the pleasure in many acts, certainly including creative acts. In the artist, the inspiration, the feeling of "having gotten it" in the nearly immortal phrase of Dr. Higgins and Eliza Doolittle, does much to inflate the self; indeed, it temporarily produces something like a manic mood—it seems like the answer to all problems for ever and a day.

The creative moment of any nature shares much with this enthusiasm, whether in businessmen or artists. For the writer or painter, the idea, the work at the moment of inspiration, is tremendously overinvested with all the Freudian units available. Even after the best creative act there is a letdown, as at the end of a love affair when all the little Freudian units of interest and love and devotion return again to eating and the other mundane affairs of living.

For the person who is neither necessarily artist nor a manic, but who goes through cycles of such experience, (and who does not, to a certain extent?) the inspirational idea seems to be the answer to all his problems. At last he will be powerful, loved, recognized as successful, wealthy —have no further problems.

Each enthusiasm is a magic answer to all his needs. And, of course, as in the nature of magic, it turns out to be a chimera, a deception. Because even if successful, no venture is the answer to all one's problems, particularly if they are internal ones rather than realistic external ones.

Nevertheless, for more people than one might care to think, living from magic to magic is a style of life. Their fictive goal is to find the magic solution for their feeling of emptiness. Since each solution fails to perform the expected miracle, they lose interest and look for the next answer to their unconscious prayer.

Of course, gamblers are of this nature, with luck as the bountiful mother and their fictive goal of love and esteem all around them. Others might expect to find just the right man or woman, and many times think they have found the one and only—as permanent as the everchanging state of permanent bliss—or at least that's what they intermittently think they have.

There are many different styles of life geared to different forms of the elusive goal of wholeness by external means. Do you know someone who seems always possessed by an intolerable drive to get innumerable things done—against all reason but for many reasons? Some individuals seem driven by the illusionary goal of finally reaching a place where their ideas will all be clear, their house all clean, their problems all taken care of. Life to them seems like so many spots to be wiped off, so many matters to be filed neatly, so many lists to be crossed off. They behave as if life could stop so that they would finally be caught up. Their obsession is to have everything under control, present and accounted for. Indeed, then they could feel that they are ten feet tall, that they are approved and loved by the nagging, critical voices of their conscience and their past. They feel life is playing them continuous tricks in not letting them gain control. Their style of living is a breathless race against the accumulation of life's excreta that threatens to engulf them. And the faster they tread, the more they stir up. The more furious they are with the world for messing up their best attempts to keep things in order, the less they feel at peace with themselves.

Others pile up millions, houses, husbands, wives, and lovers, in the hope of finding the elusive inner peace, a feeling of being somebody, of being loved, big, safe. It is this desire which makes Sammy run. It is indeed a tragedy that all the trappings of reality seem so helpless against the failings in the structure of the soul. Without a thermostat, the temperature seesaws fitfully and forever.

11

On Role Playing
as a Distance Regulator

"SOMETIMES IT MAKES you a little bit sad because you'd like to meet somebody kind of on face value. It's nice to be included in people's fantasies but you also like to be accepted for your own sake." So said Marilyn Monroe in a *Life* Magazine interview a few days before her death.

What poor Marilyn was talking about so vividly was that she had come to play a role for the world—of the beautiful but dumb blonde, of the sex bomb, and of glamorous success. Most unfortunately, that is not how she usually seems to have felt inside.

She, like so many attractive women, wanted to be loved for "herself," not for the attributes of her body. It is as if an attractive woman sees sexual attractiveness only as a very superficial role and wishes to be valued for something more "genuine." That is why it is easiest to flatter a beauty successfully by talking about how bright she is. In case

111

you are inclined to believe that intelligence is a more genuine attribute than beauty, it will be well to remember that a brilliant girl cannot be more flattered than by being considered attractive.

Marilyn Monroe, of course, seems also to have had a tremendously sensitive skin. In a world of porcupines, she felt the prick of quills when others could not perceive them.

It is not only the thinness of the psychological skin that decides how much one suffers, but also the size of the exposed area. Some saying has it that the higher the monkey climbs, the more he exposes of his derrière. The more of a public role one plays, the more area is exposed for hurts.

But that is not all. The mere difference between the public role and the private one can cause pain. The more imposing the public role, the more difficult it may be to bear the greatly different private one. Dictators and captains of industry and presidents can't always be dictators and captains and presidents. That is where the role of the crony comes in—not just for any kind of relaxation, but for the sake of a feeling of continuity, for the sake of not having to live up to the image of the public role. That is why the cronies of the great are often men from their humbler days.

Kings used to have court jesters, I suspect, for the same reason. To have at least one person who did not respect their role must have been a relief.

The role of the psychoanalyst resembles the role of the court jester, at least in that respect. After all, professors who are feared by students and colleagues, multimillionaire tycoons, imperious ladies and public idols like Marilyn

Monroe all find their way to him. With other doctors and professionals they cannot drop their role. Too often, even doctors are impressed by the status of their patients, understandably affected by their prestige and financial standing.

The psychoanalyst is in a different position for a variety of reasons. In the first place, he has to keep the identity of his patients a secret. You may have Marilyn Monroe, or a high government official, or a Nobel prize man on your couch daily, but in the ordinary course of events nobody knows about it. So vanity is largely removed because it cannot be satisfied.

The role of the psychoanalyst demands a fairly rigid performance. If he is to be of any use, he cannot kowtow, be more courteous than his job permits him, or more accommodating to one patient than to any other. The moment he does so, he interferes with the basic conditions of psychoanalytic treatment. What is more, the most outstanding personage is soon so primarily plain human in the analytic situation that most superficial considerations are likely to be forgotten most of the time.

To bear the difference between roles one plays in public and in private is only one difficulty (and of course people who are not celebrities have something of this difficulty too). The other problem is to be able to integrate the many different roles which all of us play at different stages of our lives, and often at different moments of our lives.

Growing up is both a biological process and a process of learning. Learning takes place in many forms, most of them latent and indirect. The child has to learn to behave according to the rules of each society, aside from simply acquiring a mass of information. He not only has to learn not to excrete at will but has to master many subtle roles. He has to learn what is expected of a boy, a girl, what behavior is acceptable in a wide variety of social situations. Only if one moves into a foreign culture does one become aware of the subtleties of the demands of one's own. Most American children transplanted, even temporarily, into European settings are quite at a loss for sometime.

In a way, the concept of playing one's roles appropriately (according to one's culture) could serve as an approach to the definition of normalcy. All of us play different roles every moment of our lives: as employee or employer, as a friend among friends, as father and child, perhaps as politician or teacher, even as stranger in the street. The great trick is to feel *genuine* in each one of them and not to get one role contaminated with another one. "Role playing" is not used here in the sense of playing a role in a contrived way or a dramatic performance, but rather as filling the real roles in life.

Role playing is particularly difficult when it requires the ability not to take the external forms too seriously. Take the senator, for instance, who always acts the exalted official, even if in a bar or in a theatre. In a way he is not aware that the real-life role of a senator is a limited one that is borrowed by him. Though he has to fulfill it in a particular setting, he is still plain human in most other respects, except for being mindful of some decorum, some dignity, some prerogatives in certain circumstances.

In other words, constantly staying in one role without being able to switch to the many subtly different ones in everyday life is a sign of a defect, a rigidity.

114

ON ROLE PLAYING AS A DISTANCE REGULATOR

The public never tires of hearing any form of society gossip, or any gossip for that matter, because gossip is often a look behind the stage on which the role is being played.

If a bank president typifies everything there is of respectability and stolidity, it is delicious to find that he dates a chorus girl. He has fallen out of his type-cast role, and this gives all of us comfort about some of the conflicts in our own roles.

The two different roles which everybody plays in some way may be called the public and the private—the one the world sees and the one seen only by the "valet." Many a person suffers severely from an inappropriate sense of guilt about seeming duplicity in playing vastly different roles in private and in public—even when both have a good measure of truth to them.

The more imposing the public role, the greater the upset if the private one becomes publicly known.

The most striking way of destroying the imposing public role by a very human private role was suggested by a fellow medical student. In Europe, we were particularly awed by the professor's almighty judgment at oral examinations. This fellow student suggested that we think of how the great professor would look on the chamberpot; it helped us all feel much less scared.

It is often difficult not to get one role mixed up with another. Undoubtedly, this was one of the great assets of Franklin D. Roosevelt. He could switch from the role of politician to that of President, from that of Commander-in-Chief who sorrowed with those who received posthumous medals for their dear ones to the carefree prankster or the gentleman philatelist.

Much has been said or written about how hard it is to understand Roosevelt's personality. I think he was a man with a very strong ego (in the technical, psychoanalytic sense, not in the popular one of being conceited or willful) who could master many roles without being disturbed in his basic sense of integrated oneness. He was probably a rather narcissistic personality who never gave all of himself to any of his roles and always kept a bit hidden behind a wall of emotional isolation. With this hard core, the other roles could be efficiently performed and kept from interfering with each other and disturbing the essence of his own self.

The scripts for the roles we all have to play are very subtly written and demanding. Every social situation demands a slightly different set of appropriate actions, not to be underdone or overdone. One must have just enough dim awareness of the role one plays not to get into conflict with the realistic situation. If one plays a role too consciously, one is likely to fall into the difficulties of the centipede who has to stop and wonder which leg to move next—it will hardly be a very smooth performance.

Often, role playing is interfered with by an inappropriate image of one's self. The Helen Hokinson cartoon in which the corseted, 180-pound chairlady coyly admonishes the "girls" to do their work is one version of a clash of self-image—that of a young girl—with the actual role of dowager or suburban matron.

The disturbing self-image may be on different levels of unawareness and of different degrees of pathology. One well-known professor of my acquaintance always carries himself and conducts himself as if his historian were looking over his shoulder. A swaggering adolescent obviously has the image of himself as a powerful, dangerous character; and there may be the strongly built, highly influential man who deep down thinks of himself as the little girl his mother wanted him to be. No wonder he reacts peculiarly at times to feeling misunderstood, or has to go to ridiculous extremes to impress everybody with his power—because he must hide the little girl feeling he has deep inside himself.

Mothers often get into this difficulty, if at all neurotic. The children make constant demands on them, which only increase the mother's need to be a child herself who should be pampered, or at least not imposed upon, by the children and, of course, not have demands made upon her by her husband.

Travel may well be so refreshing because it brings a change not only of external scenery but also of internal imagery. Just stepping into the plane may make one feel "like a new person" because one feels stripped of one's daily role of humdrum chores. The very anonymity as a traveler gives one a chance to play a different role. One might suspect that Americans took with such special alacrity to European travel in the post-war years because in the Continental setting they really assumed the role of the American "millionaire" which naive Europeans willingly ascribed to them.

The story is told of the famous Caliph Harun Al Raschid that he liked to mingle with his subjects in the market place, incognito, to meet his people and to reward or punish later on those unknowingly observed. There is something like an Harun Al Raschid complex in many people, especially when traveling. It finds its counterpart in the frequently burning curiosity to find out who your traveling companions are: one meets such interesting people! Your neighbor might indeed be a Caliph, or at least a mogul of business or the movies. There even are people who seem to think it fascinating to meet a psychiatrist!

Of course, travel with its change of roles also does something for the porcupine situation. The anonymity means there is rather little interaction (unless you are the one in the middle of a three-seat row on an economy flight). A trip around the world means both a chance for playing new roles and for getting some of the quills out of your skin that have given you an ulcer or a pain in one extremity or another. With a little bit of luck and a great deal of persistence, one may be able to regulate the social distances one gets involved in at a resort, whether to keep one's distance or develop a closer relationship. For example, when a woman says a man makes her feel so feminine, she means that his view of her makes her assume the role of femininity—whatever her conception (or his) of it might be. When writers of books on how to catch a husband cynically observe that the way to have him fall in love with you is to let him know that you, the girl, think he is adorable, they are usually quite right. It is not only the flattery which is effective, but the fact that the girl helps him find and play a role acceptable to himself.

There is many a Walter Mitty, or his cousin, Caspar Milquetoast, who might rise to the occasion of being a spectacular hero if faced by the proper chance to play that role. One of the few writers—or artists of any kind—that Switzerland has produced, Gottfried Keller, wrote a piece called "Kleider Machen Leute": *Clothes make the man.* One might paraphrase it and say *it's the role that makes the man.*

An acquaintance was rejected by the Army for medical reasons. Nobody was really much surprised even though the disabling condition was a relatively minor one. It was simply difficult to imagine him a soldier. He was not only the scholarly type, he had the warm, soft brown eyes of a deer and, though tall and broad, held his body so awkwardly that he appeared fragile. His legs always seemed to have independent ideas about which way to go and the effect was rather unnerving. It seemed one could hardly trust him to cross the street safely.

By one of those tortuous turns of events, he found his way into the OSS as a leader of sabotage. Against tremendously dangerous odds, he captained a small team which smuggled gold and dynamite to resistance groups behind Nazi lines, fought and hid, blasted and ambushed. He engaged in similarly hazardous tasks in the Pacific. Soon after hostilities were over, he settled down to civilian life, married an attractive girl, and took an academic job in a small college. And when you saw him walking, his legs seemed hardly able to agree on where to go and, once again, you would scarcely believe him capable of crossing a busy street without disaster. There was no manifest evidence of leadership or courage. It must have been the role that made this man now one kind of person and then another.

Indeed, that the job may make the man is well known

119

and often fortunate, or so it has been said of the American Presidency and some of the men who have held it.

Illness has a tendency to alter one's self-image strongly and the role one plays. Hospitalization is so particularly traumatic because of the enforced and tremendous difference in roles. The important business leader, the internationally-famed scholar, as well as the ordinary man or woman accustomed to run his own daily affairs, suddenly take orders even from a student nurse and are at her and everyone else's mercy, not without justified misgivings at times about their keepers' intelligence and competence.

In the hospital there is an enforced passivity which is particularly unbearable to some. Others, of course, almost joyfully take to the role of being looked after and without responsibility. Chronic illness, particularly, has this tendency to bring out in us the child who would just as soon be taken care of. A certain reluctance to take on again all the burdens of ordinary life may develop.

This self-care becomes especially striking when one organ is diseased. In the first place, one develops a new awareness of that organ, an unrealistic image even in the minds of sophisticated people. The organ acquires a relationship to the rest of the body much as New York relates to the rest of the United States in those maps supposed to present the New Yorker's image of the United States. The body seems mostly liver, or heart, or stomach, as the United States seems to consist mostly of New York. After a while, one is likely to say, "My stomach makes me do this or that." The stomach appears to become an independent being that tyrannizes or needs care, as the case may be. Indeed, part of the self-image seems to have been split off into an organ-image related symbiotically to the former. The stomach seems to have taken on a role of its own.

Another difficult change of roles has to do with aging, and specifically with retirement. The change of self-image is difficult for all, depresses some, and literally kills a few.

The least fortunate may be those who never seem to find the role that suits them. Time and place and chance may well determine the role one plays. Or so the familiar story would have it of the old soldier who came to heaven and asked St. Peter if he could show him the greatest general in all history. St. Peter took him to a corner of heaven and showed him a grizzled old man. "He is the greatest general of all time? But I know this man, he was only our village cobbler!" "Yes," said St. Peter, "but if he had been a general, he would have been the greatest of them all."

12

Some Cultural Distance Regulators

LIFE IS A PROCESS of optimal adaptation to circumstances. Though personal history is an important determi-
nant of one's behavior, the matrix of one's culture, one's
social setting, shapes much of the external forms. This
is true for profound social mores such as sexual taboos as
well as for relatively superficial ones as the correct dinner
conversation in some culture or subculture.

In the American culture, or rather in a certain middleclass subculture within it, the cocktail-party type of social
relationship, slightly past its heyday, constitutes a certain
form of social adaptation. It is largely the outgrowth of a
technology that permits and necessitates a great deal of
some kind of interaction with many people. Cocktail parties are designed to provide a seemingly friendly and close
contact with a great many people with whom, in fact, one
has only a tangential relationship. With the help of al-

cohol's ability to resolve inhibitions and judgment, and by means of established forms of role playing, one may call a great number of people familiarly by their first name whose last name one cannot remember.

It is, nevertheless, a mistake to think of cocktail parties as socially deceitful in the sense of being very craftily staged. They often involve the manifestation of very genuine personality facets. The woman whom reality has forced to act the role of mother and wife and business woman may show the girlish coquetry that is usually deeply repressed, and the solid citizen, businessman, or professional may gossip and show off, as he cannot afford to at other times.

At the cocktail party, one can permit different features of one's personality to emerge because one knows the occasion is shortlived, from five to seven, or therabouts. One can establish relationships, even communicate intimately, because it will soon be over, and chances are that one will not see the same person again or at least not for some time. When the doors close after the last drink, they usually close on the whole episode.

There are some people for whom cocktail party type of interaction is one form of relationship among many they can adapt to and enjoy. They have a choice. There are other people for whom cocktail sociability is the best form of human relationship and the only one in which they flourish. Their skin-deep charm does not make great demands on their ability to give of themselves or take in anybody else for too long a time. Their social relations are like those of the bees to the flowers—transitory. They get some honey in fermented form and a social pleasantry.

They may contribute some cross-pollination of ideas or gossip or business.

Too often, this type of sociability is mistaken for real interaction. In psychiatric histories, the fact that someone has been president of his college class, a good mixer, must not be mistaken for a criterion of good human relations. When one expresses surprise at such a person's emotional disturbances, it is really due to the fact that one mistook superficial tangential relations for those more mature ones which are more stable and not always directly gratifying.

The fact is that many people need contact with others as a form of self-affirmation, a way of maintaining or confirming their own identity. Instead of *I think, therefore I am*, their credo might be put: *I exist as Joe Jones for Jim and Mary, therefore I am*. It certainly has been said for actors that they feel real only to the extent to which they are "on stage" for the audience.

Not feeling quite real is a problem to many people at one time or another, and need not even be of any serious nature. Of course, many circumstances may interfere with the clarity of being oneself: waking suddenly from a deep sleep to strange surroundings, or the many facets of modern living with its fast changes, not only geographically, but technologically and socioeconomically.

Much more important than these external sources of alienation are internal ones. The main root of a feeling of aloneness is a lack of real closeness to anyone.

To live within oneself, self-centered even if manifestly sociable, is very difficult. It seems to lead to some problems of psychological stagnation. Having all one's interest vested in oneself makes one as vulnerable as a miser who keeps all his horde under his mattress. He hardly dares venture forth and constantly has to worry about the safety of his fortune. A very self-centered person similarly has to worry constantly about how he is feeling, what his state of mental and physical health is. The accumulation of all the emotional interest in oneself seems to lead to some sort of emotional constipation that is often felt as vague discomfort, restlessness, and boredom. It does seem as if emotional well being would depend upon a free flow of investment of interest in ideas and other people. The returns on that investment are participation and affection from others much as financial well being depends upon a judicious circulation and use of one's money, rather than having it all sewn up in the proverbial sock. A thoroughly self-centered person reminds one of nothing so much as the ingenious pictures which appeared in a series of advertisements for a bank; they show a man chained by golden links to a tremendous, man-sized egg, in a variety of impossible situations, such as in a canoe, etc. with the caption: "Unshackle yourself."

The one who treats himself as his own nest egg is self-centered as a form of self-care. He plays mother for himself because he feels nobody else did or will. Others may be self-centered—in the sense of not letting others come too close to them—because they are afraid close contact may hurt. A girl who has been disappointed in love may not want to become involved with a man again because she is afraid she might be hurt again; a child of a divorcée who has had many substitute fathers finally stops involving herself with the current one, afraid of again losing hoped-for security as in each preceding fiasco.

THE PORCUPINE DILEMMA

What is a normal relationship to people? Above all, it is a *variable* one. If one had to define psychological normality briefly, the main criterion might well be flexibility, adaptability and relative *freedom of choice of behavior*. Emotional disorders limit the choice of responses. It is one thing to *have* to keep all one's social relations in a superficial key; it is another to *choose* to do so with some. One should neither have to relate in an intimate way only with one's family or with people whom one has known all one's life, nor have to be a social butterfly. Both forms of behavior should be *possible*.

One other aspect of a healthy relationship to people— or to goals and ideas for that matter—must also be that it not serve only immediate gratifications. The man who loves a woman only because she is pretty or gratifying, or who has friends only because they are good connections, uses his relations merely as a means to an end.

It is a curious feature of human nature that "detour behavior" and delay of gratification is so often necessary and, at the same time, the only way that leads to more lasting and deeper gratification. By and large, we think of the gourmet as a more satisfied person than the gourmand. While children stuff themselves on impulse, often with ill effect, adults wait and choose their dinner carefully, if they have a chance to do so. The same is true for one's relationship to people and to broader goals. Really gratifying human relations generally develop only slowly, are savored, and last beyond the immediate purpose they serve. Even if an old friend is of no social advantage, one normally enjoys the friendship because one has become part of the other and is happy about the relationship per se rather than considering what practical end it may serve.

The problem of relating with optimal distance and degree of emotional involvement is not only important in relationship to people, but also in relationship to ideas, ideals, and goals.

The best interest of an individual may be quite in contrast to the interests of society. Many people who are maximally involved in an idea, in some work, even in other people, destroy themselves in the process. The revolutionary who is killed while freeing the population from a tyrant, the artist who starves to produce creations which will transport others, the scientist who risks his life—they have not found the optimal porcupine index in personal terms. If they are successful, posterity hails them for their sacrifice. If they fail, their oddity is gravely recorded.

To be "adjusted," to give just enough without too much pain from the prick of quills, has in a way become a cultural ideal. The smoothest performer of them all may not be the ideal, however.

One probably needs to be a different distance from different people at the same time. The person who wants to be close to everyone is as disturbed as the one who keeps a distance from all. Provided one relates to somebody in a way that transcends the immediately utilitarian or instinctual, there is no reason why each of us should not have a totally different pattern of interactions.

There is room, and need in fact, for totally different modes of living. Sociometry is a branch of behavioral science which indeed attempts to gauge in a real situation, such as a factory, club, or school, how many personal contacts someone has, of what length, with how many people. For some situations it is important to select people who can stand each other in a close and intense relationship, such as in a tank or a submarine. Some social tensions are undoubtedly in part due simply to the irritating effect of too many interactions per available time and space.

The degrees of interaction and their extent do vary widely for different people. One person could not stand to be alone in a room, but he also could not tolerate to be in a room with other people. For him, the only tranquilizing action was to walk on the street, to be surrounded by passing people and yet not to be in contact with them. This was, of course, a particularly disturbed man who had been hospitalized twice. A sheltered workshop was a very helpful rehabilitative experience for him. In this special kind of factory, he was expected to work for a wage, but was surrounded by foremen who had psychological experience and who could call on a social worker and a psychiatrist to help the patient. The patient did not need to work a full day at first, since this was more social interaction with peers, superiors, and the work than he could stand. If he behaved asocially, he was not fired, but had a chance to discuss his tensions and try again. In that sense, the sheltered workshop provided a chance for trial and error, for acquiring tolerance of social interactions and their tensions, and helped him to develop a satisfactory mode of social relations even outside the immediate setting of the shop.

Particularly difficult for themselves and others are those who want to regulate social involvement by their anxieties and desires. One man had a most illuminating fantasy concerning his social relations. He wanted to have a three-story house and live on the third floor. His needs were food and books that would be supplied on a conveyor belt. He would fill the house with his friends on the first two floors and descend to them or have them ascend to his hideaway when he felt lonely, but he would not be available at *their* demand. Social relations were strictly one way —his way.

Needless to say, he was a moody person. In fact, the anxiety basic to his social relations became most clear in his steadily recurring fantasies prior to falling asleep. From childhood on he was beset by fears of being hurt. These fears had enlarged over the years. Originally, he retired in his falling-asleep fantasies to a blockhouse in the woods to be safe from other people. As time went on, this wasn't safe enough, and he put a large barbed wire fence around his fantasy domicile. As the years went by, he added machine gun nests, land mines, an electric alarm system, dogs, and watch towers. As with the rings of a tree, one could tell eventually the many years he had had this fantasy by the rings of security measures he added as he went along. Such were his fantasies for a lullaby. This was a man who could only move from "21," to the Colony, to the Stork Club, to Sardi's, where he was known for the great talent that he was. The idea of stopping at a frankfurter stand filled him with the dread of all his shyness and apprehension of meeting other people. And yet, being alone was also unbearable for him.

The burden of consciousness weighs heavily upon us. Loneliness is usually so unbearable because it increases the weight of consciousness and the press of internal stresses and concomitant anxiety. Experiments in perceptual isolation and partial sensory deprivation have shown conclusively that absence of external clues and stimuli usually produces anxiety and a threat of disorientation and a confusion of what is real and what is not.

One patient, when overcome by panic, particularly while alone, frequently smashed window panes with his bare hands. The pain of the cuts and concern about the wounds constituted a welcome relief from the turmoil within himself—a nameless panic and a feeling of not being quite real.

For others, the situation is less extreme: they like to be in special contact, without personal relations or real interaction most of the time. The cocktail party is one setting permitting this type of relationship. Some bars often flourish because they too encourage this type of relationship. At the bar in a pub or cocktail lounge, people do not face each other. Men may sit for hours without saying much. Of course, if sufficiently dissolved in alcohol, some talk, tell their troubles, or fight, but not with anyone with whom they have a permanent relationship.

The Greenwich Village bar may be a special breed of social interaction, though in some ways a precursor of the ways of hippies. There, people not only often know each other by first name, but may engage in some seemingly intimate interaction. They may lend each other shirts, or may have sexual relations, but these facts do not promote a close relationship. All interaction seems to be of a non-obligatory, non-binding nature. If one may think of some social interaction in terms of chemical reactions with more or less stable compounds, we deal in the present case with barely a physical solution. Like a measure of oil and water, there may be some interspersing, but no real union. It filters out again automatically. The remarkable fact is that this may be done without any rancor, as if it were understood as a special social contract that all relations remain very mobile. If a typical Villager makes an appointment for nine o'clock, he may turn up at ten, or eleven, or not at all, and his correspondent, likely as not, will also not appear, or simply walk away after some waiting. Take it or leave it seems to be the motto. A fear to commit oneself, an inability to forgo intercurrent desires for the sake of fulfilling an obligation is basic to this problem and its treatment.

To say that we need others for distraction from ourselves lends itself to fine cynical commentary. For most of us, adulthood brings a measure of self-sufficiency, of being contentedly a universe of our own at least some of the time. For others, the very thought of any aloneness is unbearable. They talk to strangers on trains, they are compulsive "joiners" who populate fraternal organizations and bars. Agarophobes hardly ever move away from their families and are afraid to cross the street alone. An idle hour, even with books around, threatens ennui and anguish.

Many people carry their need for brief tangential social relationships into their occupational life. Cab drivers are a prime example; these are people who often speak of their need for independence, of freedom from an office chair, and of the enclosed atmosphere of sameness. Their life as taxi drivers permits them *brief* contacts with their fares whether they talk or not. As one of them put it, "What if there is an unpleasant one? Ten minutes later

I am rid of him." Their long day consists of the shortest and slightest interactions with other people. Often, their contact with their nightman is restricted to a brief greeting, and even the cab is often not the same from day to day. There is no constancy of colleagues, customers, superiors, or scenery.

Yet, the tragicomedy, of course, is that in some ways their life has a great deal of sameness—similar traffic problems and similar fares, while the driver's seat has as much sameness as any office chair. Their personal limitations circumscribe their life much like anybody else's. Most of them have tried other careers and found themselves unable to bear them. Their life as cabbies provides them an illusion of change that is crucial for their ability to stand human relationships.

There are many situations where one can be in close proximity to people without really having to interact with them. People who cannot find such arrangements suitable to their needs often have to solve the problem of painful interaction by frequent changes of jobs and friends and even domicile. It is fairly well established that emotional disorders are more frequent in the very mobile part of the population. Relatively unstable people gravitate into a quickly shifting population. (In turn, it is quite likely that a great deal of mobility due to other than personal emotional factors may cause a weakening of a sense of identity and thus cause emotional instability.) One of the most reliable social indicators of interpersonal difficulties and especially paranoid tendencies lies in a history of frequent job changes in a person of middleclass culture. In a migratory wetback, or some other underprivileged person, the social factors are usually the determining ones, rather than individual problems.

Aside from people differing individually, there may well be national characteristics. According to the stereotype, the Englishman is cold, distant, and reserved—the Latin, warm, if not mercurial. To the extent to which such stereotypes hold true, they are subject to change over time. The English character seems to have undergone several modifications in the course of the last few decades. Such phenomena as the Beatles and the whole change of style in dress and manners are much at variance with pre-World War II characteristics. (Within a given culture, different subcultures may vary greatly; if the public school graduate was aloof, it hardly ever held true for the Cockney.)

Some generalization might be applicable supranationally. Though individuals differ, our generation tends increasingly towards shallower emotions to each other. Hippies constitute an exception and a reaction to that trend, but only to a certain extent. While proclaiming the importance of love, their emotional relationships are actually very loose and shallow.

Modern technology may offer some relief to those who prefer many and loose relations. With increased international interdependence, greater social mobility, better means for travel and a favorable economy, there is more chance for putting distance between oneself and what bothers one.

Some may indeed become more disturbed in the crowded quarters of the city because there is too much close interaction all the time. Others may like to live in the city because one can always be close to people, albeit impersonally. In the big city with its anonymity, the superficial interactions with many people may provide the distance necessary for the comfort of some people. After all, inhabitants of small communities often seem to be shareholders in a set of paranoid preoccupations with each other.

What may seem like wintry isolation in the impersonal life of the city to one may be a lovely semi-private beach to another.

Schopenhauer lived before the time of Freud, before the invention of the automatic rangefinder and before the discovery of the thermostat built into house and man—or else he might have recommended these handy gadgets to his porcupines.

13

Of Men, Women, and Marriage

DISRAELI IS REPORTED to have said that every country has the Jews it deserves. In a variation, one might say that every husband has the wife he deserves, and vice versa.

Of course, Disraeli had been instrumental in adding India to the crown of his beloved queen and arranged the acquisition of the then vital Suez Canal. He obviously felt that England deserved the best of Jews, such as himself. Husbands and wives generally feel *they* deserve the best of mates. The most miserable character whom nobody can stand and who cannot get along with anybody may complain that it is difficult to get along with *women!* Or maybe he will be more specific and merely complain how hard it is to get along with a wife.

The difficulties of marriage have wrongly or inaccurately been ascribed to the problems of a man and woman living together in close proximity. Without underestimating the importance of sex, it is likely that most marital difficulties are due to two *people* having to live closely together.

Marriage is simply one type of close human relationship which has a great deal in common with the difficulties of all other close and intense human relationships, regardless of sex.

In marriage, the chances for impinging annoyingly on each other are infinite. It starts with the morning's struggle not to interfere with each other too badly in the necessary rituals of launching into the day. It ends with chances for irritation over such simple matters as a suitable time for turning out the light. Between these two events, there are infinite possibilities for rubbing each other the wrong way with regard to predilections—and their timing —of sex, food, conversation, or TV programs; or, as the case may be, over friends, money, and the relationship to the children, to mention just a bare minimum. The remarkable fact is that it apparently can be endured.

Partners in research, or the crew of an armored tank outfit, or literary collaborators very often get into difficulties with each other. Those who do not, such as Rodgers and Hammerstein, become legends. A close complementary and supplementary relationship between two or more people is difficult. Chances are that the people who habitually have difficulties in their marital relationship have more difficulties than the next person in other human relations. There are exceptions to this rule, most notably in those cases where someone lived rather happily before marriage, and not immediately afterwards. The most dramatic are those instances where a couple has lived happily together—sexually and otherwise—but one of the partners becomes depressed or sexually malfunctioning *after* the legal wedding. In such instances, the marriage vow may have a specific symbolic meaning which becomes the source of a disturbance, or the feeling of legal obligation may be too much to bear or may remove the feeling of romance.

There are people for whom any kind of close relationship is hard to bear, who have managed life without it— until marriage is forced upon them by our cultural pressures. Then they find that "marriage does not agree with them," when in truth one would have to say that "a close relationship does not agree with them." There are, of course, others who can bear a marriage that does not become a close relationship in emotional, geographic, or other ways.

Much of the nature and fate of a marital relationship is probably determined (and can be observed and understood often by all but the people involved) *in the very first encounter of two people.* Again, this is hardly unique to the marriage relationship. If one carefully observes the habitual role someone plays—and the responses he elicits— from such brief transactions as are involved with shop clerks, waiters, and other transitory actors of daily life, one will find that subtle factors of voice, bodily hearing, and various attitudes will produce individually characteristic effects, often unbeknown to both actors, within seconds of meeting. They immediately start taking certain roles in relation to each other.

From the first moment on, a series of mostly unconscious cues determine a process of mutual *role-taking* which not only structures the future relationship, but also involves a complex interaction of accepting and rejecting maneuvers. These cues belong not only to the actual looks of the other person, but to his voice, his stance and general bearing, and his response to the other person's cues. One can see in less than five minutes or five sentences a person who has related to John in an assertive way relate to Jim in a passive, dependent way, in the absence of any previous acquaintance or difference of status.

"Love at first sight" is a popular conception of the occasional event when a person becomes forcefully aware of another's perfect fit to his expectations, even though he is consciously unaware of what actually determines the fit. As we all know, this perfect "fit" is frequently not a lasting one. The situation may be structured at the moment of encounter so as to fit the second person's innermost needs—e.g., a man in the role of hero to the maiden in distress, or the older man who resembles father just enough and not too much to constitute an ideal image for the adolescent girl. There are many determinants of one's choice and, of course, object relations and role playing may undergo and bring about some mutual changes.

In a surprising number of relationships, the mutual roles taken at the first encounter remain essentially the same in years to come. The vantage point of the psychoanalyst, of course, affords chances for studying situations in *statu nascendi* as well as in retrospect. Since many patients are in their twenties and unmarried when they first come to analysis, and since analysis takes several years, there is, simply on an actuarial basis, a frequent occasion for studying the interaction of two people from the first chance meeting to possible later fruition in marriage. (The excellent analytical rule that patients should ordinarily not marry while in analysis, or at least not until the one particular relationship has been thoroughly analyzed, has, of course, its basis in the fact that analysts know that choices of mates are influenced by the constituents of one's own personality, and that these constituents and, therefore, the choices, are influenced by the analytic process. Since many infantile trends are revived during analysis, personal interests established during analysis may be of a transitory nature. Thus, the patient must be guarded against rash decisions.)

Analysis is the ideal situation not only for studying personal relations, but also for studying changes in choices as therapeutic changes take place in a person. Furthermore, it frequently affords occasion to observe that changes in one person, due to therapy, may bring about changes in the other person—simply by changing the cues the first person represents to the second one, and by altering the responses of the first person to the second's cues. For instance, when a very masochistic, but quietly nagging, wife who was completely exploited by a narcissistic, demanding, inconsiderate husband changed to being less self-harming, less nagging, the husband became more considerate and attentive without any specific discussion of the matters concerned—as if by magic. What had changed were perceptual cues and responses which neither of the partners was consciously aware of, but were perfectly apparent to the analyst, and for that matter, to friends and family members of the patient. In their middle thirties at the time of treatment, this couple had met in their very early teens and married before they were twenty. The essentials of their roles had existed in the very first encounter and lasted up to the time of the therapeutic changes. In the course of treatment, it became quite clear that the future husband was chosen in the image of the patient's own demanding, self-centered mother.

Any one of a number of meaningful relationships in a person's life may influence his own personality and the role he plays and the cues he responds to in others. A governess or maid may at times play as much of a determining role as a mother; so may a sister, or a cousin. Of course, much as we are all composites of identifications with a variety of people in our life (and the whole adds up to something more than the simple sum of the parts— namely, a unique configuration), so the cues we respond to in other people are also composites. For that matter, of course, features of persons of the same sex—a father, brother, or other person—may enter into the cues that make a member of the opposite sex attractive or repulsive without involving any question of homosexuality.

Negative criteria may also play a role. Dependent upon the *perceived* relationship of the parents (which may be quite different from the "real" relationship as perceived by a majority of others), a girl may have the conscious, preconscious, or unconscious mental set: "I am not going to marry a tyrant like daddy." In an extreme case, such a girl may identify herself with father and marry a man who will be as much a dishrag to her as her own mother was to her father. A number of other characteristics may also be more of the masculine variety in the case of this woman and more feminine in her mate.

Any number of psychological traits may become the basis for "cueing" and role-taking. Some people may "find" each other because they are similarly self-centered and can stand only a minimal contact. Others like to sit in each other's lap, emotionally speaking. Schopenhauer's story of the porcupines applies here—e.g., consider the fact that some people marry knowing very well that the husband will have to spend much time away, as with a salesman, actor, or sailor. In an isolated fishing community the social conditions are more important determining factors than psychological choice. In most other circumstances, however, it is extremely likely that what may appear as a drawback—frequent, often prolonged, separation—may actually be a necessary prerequisite for making a relationship bearable for both. On the other hand, occasionally scientists, writers or business people may marry and not only be mature collaborators, but actually live so close together as to create a virtual symbiosis. Sometimes, one friend will think that he is dependent on her and another friend may feel that it is the other way round. In the example we have in mind, the fact is that they are mutually interdependent, for better or worse. It may well be that the woman shows dash and even aggression, for instance, but close examination may show that she is able to behave this way because the husband provides the quiet, even retiring, strength which makes it possible for her to function that way—or vice versa, of course. Only if either of the partners periodically withdraws support, or uses either role for denigration of the other one, need such a relationship be harmful.

Otherwise, they may live happily ever after—until one of them dies. Then one-half of a living organism is indeed all that remains.

In marriage, too, the porcupine index plays a role. The amount of psychological distance one prefers may determine the choice and structure of marital life. The distance could have periodic cycles, of course: periods of closeness interchanged with periods of distance.

Some people choose a partner for virtual symbiosis, others for a joint venture in parasitism, for mutual leaning upon each other, or for various forms of complementation and supplementation. Of course, much of this behavior is well within normal limits. Often a very good relationship may be established by mutual identification with each other to a point where they are truly "part of each other" and, in a way, transcend the form of relationship where one only means as much to each other as one can give each other; in such a relationship, a middle-aged husband may not be less fond of his wife because she has aged, and the wife may love him with all the limitations she has become aware of.

Modern marriage may be the most difficult kind because it probably expects more intricate compatibility on more levels than was the case at any other time. Before the emancipation of women, the expectations were greatly limited by the master-chattel role. Marriages were arranged as a matter of accommodation. Now, intellectual harmony must be matched by synchronous orgasms. The means which different couples find for diluting the forces of interaction vary culturally and personally. Modern travel or the exigencies of business serve for some—sisterhood evenings, bowling, golf, canasta or bridge evenings for others.

For many, marriage is still a matter of accommodation. Simply to have attained the status fulfills a certain social expectation and the canons of "normality," and the degree of relatedness thereafter may be absolutely minimal. It may still involve a certain amount of protection against loneliness, and some comfort in illness, but that is often all. I am sure there would be many surprises if a census were available on the emotional and sexual relations in marriage. There seems to be an abundance of husbands who fall asleep in their clothes at the television set and never manage to get to bed in time. There are some characterized by the unduly passive role of the husband and the assertive masculine role of the wife. Often enough they essentially, and unconsciously, play children together, dedicated to the fulfillment of their own or their mutual infantile needs. To be fed and otherwise looked after in his personal comforts by the wife may be the husband's satisfaction; to be able to indulge in the equivalent of dollplay, in the form of home decorating, and the equivalent of candy-store freedom, in the form of a charge account, may be the wife's real pleasure.

One woman who used to suffer from panics in her childhood when her parents were away from home had her husband simply fulfill the role of a person to be there, to keep her from feeling unbearably anxious.

Another woman grew up in great awe and dread of her father. Her childhood fantasies were often filled with ideas of armies advancing on her. There were always brutal men endangering her. Subtly, it became apparent that sometimes she would really feel as if she were one of the men. It became more comfortable to feature herself as one of the aggressors rather than the victim. In adult life, she found herself men, and eventually husbands, who had features of both marked assertiveness, if not aggression, and passivity. It did not matter which was the manifest and which the hidden trait. Sooner or later she would be rather passive, helpless, and even victimized, only then to turn and become the aggressive one. After a while, she would be scared of her own aggressive desires and switch again to the former role. It made for rather turbulent relations. The fact is, of course, that a certain degree of this dual quality is quite common. Boys will run after girls and pull their hair, and the girls may giggle but slap the boys when it gets out of hand. This is a form of flirtation and, as teasing, or *roughhousing*, finds its way into adult sexual foreplay or actual activity. In the case of the woman discussed, the need for aggression and passivity was excessive. In many other marriages, with a somewhat similar struggle over who is "on top," the most minute daily event may become a battleground—for it is not whether the soup was warm or cold, the turn with the automobile right or wrong, but rather who is dishing it out and who is taking it. Almost anything lends itself as material for that sort of struggle, if that is one's problem. It is virtually impossible to play this alone, and usually both partners have fairly even doses of the problem.

The first meeting, as we said, is a nuclear event. In it all the determinants of personalities come into immediate play. There is no question, however, that different facets may emerge in differing degrees at different times, and that a time factor may be built into the unrolling of certain personality characteristics. For instance, a woman may at first always be fascinated by a man's outstandingly superior qualities. While she is full of genuine admiration in the beginning, later this situation may make her a little competitive as she feels threatened by his "superiority." In men interested in competition, this may lead to a prolongation of the relationship; in a masochistic man, with a woman characterized by a wish to be more active and aggressive, the permanent, outstanding pattern may gradually *become* a relationship to this passive nature of the male. If the same woman should happen to be "cued in" initially with a man structured so as to want to continue in the active role, the woman may leave him for another partner, or he may lose interest in her and break off. With enough of a wish to be passive in the same woman, she may forgo most of her need for dominance and accept the passive role in relation to this man.

Thus, it is quite true that either maxim may hold true for different people, or sometimes for the same person: *"gleich und gleich gesellt sich gerne"* (people of identical nature like to keep company), or *"opposites attract each other."* Psychoanalysts hold opposite poles to be closely related: a masochist is merely a sadist towards himself, and a sadist often behaves masochistically in some other facet of his life.

The stability and pervasiveness of a pattern of relationship provide for a great many variations. A woman who may settle for one kind of a relationship to one man may need to change to the opposite relationship with another man—e.g., there may be in some of the most stable

145

relationships a compromise situation: the man adopts certain attitudes in some areas—and the woman, certain attitudes in other areas. For simplicity's sake, we might use again the overworked example of activity and passivity. In many families the woman plays the more active, determining role in social situations, the man in other situations. This, incidentally, has often led to the false generalization that the "wife wears the pants." Such an interaction may be entirely misleading. For instance, the man may be the one to give emotional support and structure to the marriage in situations other than social ones. The same, of course, may hold true for the reverse situation: many a man who seems like a tyrant in the social setting may indeed be emotionally supported by his wife in every other situation.

It is very often true in our culture that the man expends nearly all his interest, as well as his need and ability for controlling situations and people in his work sphere and thus leaves the domestic, social, and even cultural areas to the wife. Whether this is apparently more so in the American culture because the working life for professionals, businessmen, and everybody else absorbs so much more of the competitive spirit than in other cultures is an interesting speculation. If so, it would not be true—as has often been said—that American women are more aggressive; it would only hold true that in certain situations American women have to be so much more aggressive than women in other cultures because their mates have to be so much more aggressive in their working life than other males.

Speaking of culture, one should not fail to mention that any number of sociological and anthropological cues decide the choice of mates, often largely without conscious awareness of the participants. The major aspects of religion, socioeconomic factors, ethnic background, and color consciously enter into choice. Much of the cueing is determined and realistically influenced by the circles one moves in.

On the other hand, biological factors such as energy level, size, intellectual and artistic endowment and sexual attributes play a sometimes subtle, and other times clearly perceptible, role.

In marriage, premenstrual time is crisis time. It is at this time that the lady of the house is likely to grow her real winter coat of luxurious quills and, paradoxically, a hypersensitive skin at the same time. There is almost certainly no other single factor as much responsible for marital discord as premenstrual tension. The worst of it all is that the significance of this time bomb, regularly discharged on a lunar calendar, often remains entirely unknown to both spouses, even in sophisticated households. It just happens, it seems, that a quarrel breaks loose over anything at all. Time and again I have found on checking carefully over several years of analysis that the one common element was premenstrual time—no matter what the seeming reason. This has been so reliable an indicator that I would often ask if the woman were not premenstrual only to be informed that the period was two weeks off, or ten days. At the next visit, it would turn out that the mood was a more reliable indicator than the calendar itself.

There are some physiological reasons for the increased porcupine index, and the more pronounced these are, the more likely that there will be trouble. Without going into the complex endocrine processes, it will suffice to say that water retention plays a large role. Even for a healthy, normal woman it is not unusual to have a weight difference of four pounds between the day before menstruation and the day the flow starts. Many times, the weight gain before menstruation, almost exclusively of water diffusely present in the tissues, is responsible for troubled situations. The clothes are too tight, the breasts uncomfortably heavy, the very skin seems too tight, a general feeling of loginess prevails. Most significant for the raw temper may be the fact that the meninges, the lining of the brain, are also waterlogged, and that this condition may produce irritation of the brain which quite logically leads to an irritation of the marital situation.

There may be, in addition, psychological reasons for irritability: infantile misconceptions concerning the bleeding, imagined injury or castration, feeling of loss of control over what seems like an excretion. To the extent to which these factors play a role, wifely aggression may indeed be a form of vengeance, defense, and denial.

Be that as it may, the best advice to any newly-wed couple might well be: keep an accurate calendar of the red letter days and stay aware of them. Then discount any tempers that occur at least from the twenty-sixth day on, and marriage may be a significantly smoother affair!

It is obvious, then, that psychological determinants do not exist in a vacuum but interact circularly with many other factors. Not only is marriage but one kind, one variation, of a human relationship; it is a relationship within the matrix of complex biological and cultural forces pulling one hither and yon.

One could hardly think of a better illustration of the Schopenhauer parable than the marriage bed. A cynic, in fact, would have it that marriage is very much like social welfare provisions, designed to meet some basic human needs: both institutions provide enough to make them a necessity, but not enough to make them worthwhile.

14

To Be Aware or Not Aware

WITH THE SUNDAY MORNING coffee a review of
Marcel Proust's biography. His pursuit into things past
. . . "Temps perdu" sounds much better for this sample
of the human tragicomedy: the neurotic son of a physician
(who had been an authority on hygiene) engaged in a
most unhygienic search for the meaning of life, oversensi-
tive to nearly everything. If one were to believe the biog-
rapher—and I don't—a single episode of his mother's re-
fusal of a good night kiss brought about Proust's lifelong
obsession with love and jealousy.

How nice it must be not to be a clinician and to see
simpler relationships between cause and effect. In fact,
being a clinician has spoiled much of the enjoyment of

literature. Even if there is no quarrel to pick technically, writing sometimes seems two-dimensional compared to the drama in the consulting room. Paradoxically, literature seems too fussy and complex at other times; it is difficult to accompany Proust into his exploration of his personal hell of homosexual hypersensitivities, his precious examination of the comic foibles of the people around him.

And yet, it is not so simple a matter. I have felt the same way about Dostoevsky and Tennessee Williams as I do about Proust. It is strange that I can indeed spend many hours a day listening with genuine interest to some of the smallest details of neurotic troubles of patients and yet become impatient with sensitive writers. I feel like saying to them: For God's sake get on with it! Stop the emoting, the examining. A bit of analysis and a healthy affair could fix it.

I almost believed that myself, until I turned the page of the *Times* to a review of the speeches of General Douglas MacArthur. The counterpoint did it. The soldier speaks with certitude (but then I have had people with certitude in treatment also).

The Prousts, Camus, Williamses and Dostoevskys are involved full time in what the rest of us—including the self-sure soldiers—feel only at certain times, when the noise and rush of the daily hubbub are muted, in mourning or in love, in illness or in solitude. To the extent to which they help us understand and help us share the human situation, they do something constructive for us.

It is tragicomical, again, that many writers come to understand human relationships to a large extent by abstaining from them. In the solitude of their excessive suffering they experience in pure culture the pains of human interaction. Could a Proust have engaged in his complex searches for understanding if the demands of a suburban family had been upon him? It takes such a writer's exquisite narcissism to make our wood and field variety of self more understandable.

In that sense the writer permits us to enrich our lives by participating in the lives of his creatures. Reading becomes trial action. In the more banal sense, one may enjoy learning about the lives and mores of other cities, other cultures. In great literature, we find a reflective mirroring of ourselves, if often in a strange and grossly distorting mirror. One of the more fascinating facets of this symbiosis between writer and reader is that his own ability to experience and to communicate rarely does the writer himself any good, if one means by "good" that he lives a more serene life. One might almost paraphrase Shaw's observation: those who know how, live—those who can't, write.

The one experiment none of us can perform is to live life over again, learning from our mistakes, or simply taking a different path—if we could. In the novel, we can live many peoples' lives. To the extent to which the novel explores life, we can engage in trial action, in trial role playing. I think that fact alone may explain the enduring fascination with literary products throughout the ages.

Maybe this viewpoint might also help understand why some literature is apparently "great" while other writings are limited in time and appeal. One could try to set up an equation between greatness and the multiplicity of experiences, trial action and temporary roles a work of fiction permits.

There are of course the works which offer pleasant balm, and are like a welcome anesthetic, or at least an analgesic like an aspirin. In romantic novels, they permit us to play attractive roles and allow vicarious titillation. Moreover, there are qualities of structure in the work of fiction which greatly improve on life. The popular novel, or the detective story has to move. Not only does it progress (unlike so many situations in life), but we are safely led over increasing tension to the certainty of resolution. The hero gets the heroine, the wrongdoer is apprehended, the detective survives. Though there is obviously much simple drive gratification, the crux of the great appeal, especially in mysteries, may lie in structure. Tension is pleasant if we know it will not become overwhelming and will in due course be resolved. In that case, fiction creates a little model—an analogy of what we would like life to be. In the model we can experience the satisfaction which so often we cannot obtain in real life: closure, a sense of completion.

In resolving the artificial tension produced by the writer we seem to reduce simultaneously some of the tension of our real lives. The detective story, in that sense, serves as a decompression chamber. It provides some transition from the pressures of the day to the relaxation of the evening via its service as a scale model.

As detective fiction has become less two-dimensional providing deeper character sketches and something more than a puzzle and its solution, it has moved into the area of "good" literature. Spies who are in or out of the cold are a lot more believable, reflecting ourselves. To the extent to which they do that, they defeat some of the purpose of what has rightly been called escape literature. On that basis I predict a short life for this type of work.

For everybody needs some type of vacation from awareness. Awareness is the inner porcupine spines. Maybe people need literature which increases their full awareness if they don't have enough awareness in the course of their daily life. Often a businessman in a group of scholars seems the only one interested in talking intellectually. The humanists and social scientists and writers are talking about the best paint to use on the barn.

I think the moral of the story is to use awareness-expanding literature as cautiously as such consciousness-expanding drugs as LSD and Mexican mushroom poisons. Maybe it's all right for Huxley and the likes of him, because his only business, his only concern, is his own awareness— and letting us know about it. For the rest of us, those who have to get on with living, too much literary awareness might give us as much of a headache as too much of any good thing. Too little of it may also be serious, of course.

Consider, too, some famed literary characters. They suffer from what they try to palm off on us—too much awareness. Whether it is Hamlet's doubts, Marquand's flashbacks, the storm-tossed heroes of stream of consciousness writing, or even Saul Bellows' poor old Moses Herzog —they have too much of a good thing. Herzog constantly writes letters in his mind, when he should attend to his wife, the suit salesman or his mistress. I suppose these types write imaginary letters while making love or, more prosaically, stay aware of the ticking of the clock, the noise of traffic and the awkward posture of their legs.

A little selective inattention, a little suspension of disbelief, a bit of dramatic illusion—in short, a little less awareness—and we might all be better off.

The line between egghead and squarehead is a tenuous one. One should not have to be either, but *have a choice*—be able to be either, as the circumstances demand. That way lies some kind of happiness. The better one is able to switch on and switch off awareness, the better off one is. The more automatically the switch works, the better yet.

The book review permits a switching on and off—with the heroes and back to the writer. In that way, the book review is more satisfying than fiction itself. It serves a smorgasbord of literary nurture. It permits us vicarious role playing with the writer by enabling us to see the relationship of his real life to his work. He becomes fictional material himself and we marvel at the human frailty of some of the giants who have moved and enriched generations.

For surely, their life is no answer to life. They may well have understood the finiteness, the despair, the irony of life and its essential lack of meaning. But the only way to give meaning to life—at least subjective meaning—is to live it actively and probably less neurotically, with less perceptiveness; not with the blind certitude of a squarehead who misses all nuances and sensitivity for a dubious kind of armistice, but rather with the life-affirmative attitude of the egghead who knows there is nothing to affirm and the only salvation lies in being aware of that fact and managing to live affirmatively at the same time. The intermittent, willing suspension of disbelief is the key to the enjoyment of drama, on and off the stage.

15

The Vital Delusions as
Pain Killers

THE NEED for relative freedom from the social and emotional impact of others, while having a measure of comfort from some closeness, is only one aspect of human needs.

A similar need for the feeling of freedom of action, with some available comfort from specific ideas of support of those actions, exists in the seemingly more abstract world of the mind itself. It seems we all like the idea that we are free: free to act without impingement of others, free of limitations of our own mortality, free from inborn limitations, and free from the limitations of causality, or any determining forces in whatever form they may come.

Such notions seem a correlate to the psychological need for some distance from others. Like the porcupine index in social relations, different people seem to have differing needs for degrees of such freedom. The main regulation of comfort/distance seems to take place by complicated forms of self-deception.

Indeed, some come to cozy arrangements with the forces that they otherwise prefer to insist do not exist. While preferring to feel that they can act freely and are even willing to take the consequences of moral freedom to act, they willingly accept the idea of a divinity which comes in helpfully, rewardingly, or punitively under certain circumstances. If the divine or fateful forces seem uncomfortable and closely impinging, they reserve some elbow room with the concept that good and proper behavior will suitably influence divine handling of their fate —by prayer, good deeds, etc. That way it is not a coldly deterministic world, and yet one that provides some warmth of a supernatural, parental power. For the Greeks and others, such power was more fraternal at times than paternal, and mere saints are sometimes treated on more personal terms in Christian mythology.

Long before Freud a Viennese operetta, "Die Fledermaus," celebrated the general usefulness of the defense mechanism of repression and denial: *Gluecklich ist wer vergisst was nicht mehr zu ändern ist* (Lucky he who forgets what can't be changed.)

Yet, psychiatry usually relates denial to emotional illness. The patient sweeping the floor in the mental hospital who maintains he is the first astronaut to have returned from walking on the moon denies his illness and his confined life.

The intelligent man who is not quite sure whether he inherited fifty thousand or five hundred thousand dollars from his father excessively denies his greed and his guilt because of it.

There are transitions from emotional illness to health. A hunter lost in the wilderness who hallucinates water and food denies his predicament in a way that may help him carry on until a successful rescue. A patient deathly ill with a stomach cancer may deny the meaning of radiation treatment and manage to waste away fairly serenely insisting that he will recover from this ulcer.

In fact, some denial and "selective inattention" belong to daily life. Without ignoring disturbing external and internal stimuli there can be no normal functioning.

Life is only bearable if one is unaware of some basic facts of life, almost to the point of having delusions: false beliefs maintained in spite of evidence to the contrary.

Suicide may occur when people cannot engage in denial and repression necessary to maintain the vital delusions. Suffering, as a consequence of low self-esteem and disappointment, plays a significant role in their act.

Schopenhauer, unhappy and pessimistic, had to invent the idea of "the blind will to live" to explain the phenomenon of clinging to life, especially in clearly hopeless circumstances. While most lives are by no means as melancholy as Schopenhauer's was, he had a point. It need not take any mystical drive beyond the ordinary biological forces, however, to explain the motivation to go on living. Denial is explanation enough. Depressed people like Schopenhauer see the limitations of life more clearly than others, though they exaggerate and distort, to their own detriment. Their misfortune lies in a psychological constellation that makes them unable to maintain the vital delusions. Their relations to others are not good enough to permit them to enjoy the limited gratifications available to the rest of us.

Four vital delusions are essential to maintaining a *bearable* life. They are the delusion of *immortality*, the youthful delusion of *unlimited possibilities* in the development of one's life, the delusion of *freedom of will and action.* Underlying them all is the delusion of an *attainable state of bliss,* be it as permanent orgasm or as heaven. In practice, these four delusions are often inseparable and interlocking.

By the delusion of *immortality*, I do not mean anything philosophical or religious, but simply that *we usually live by the premise that we will continue to live.* It seems impossible to live without planning for tomorrow and later. The person who wonders constantly whether he will indeed be alive tomorrow is hampered in his actions. The ceiling may, of course, fall at any moment, but the probability is not great enough to keep worrying about this or similar possibilities—or else life just passes us by. We all behave most of the time *as if* there were *no end at all, as if* we did not notice the limitations within which our lives are likely to run out.

How valuable the vital delusion of immortality can be is best shown in situations of danger. Such a belief helps one transcend the immediate reality with courage, dignity, or sometimes obliviousness. A good example of the uses of denial of mortality exists in the soldier who feels that death is something that happens to the *other* fellow. Fatalism is a derivative of this vital delusion: no use worrying—there is only one bullet that has one's number.

To a considerable extent, we all live by the notion that

it can't happen to us. Much of the shattering effect which the death of one near to us has, or even of an accident merely geographically near, is that it explodes the protective armor of denial. It makes it a little more difficult to maintain this vital delusion.

We do not usually think of *life* in concrete form with a beginning and an end. The essence of life lies in living. We are engaged in the *process*. That is why the race driver, the youth in love, and the explorer are able to take joyous risks—and sometimes bring us progress. On the other hand, it makes it possible for the coolie, and all the coolies among us, to plod along, with not much solace or comfort, as if there were plenty of time for a better life to come.

Increasing age makes the maintenance of this vital delusion progressively more difficult. As the joints ache with arthritis, it is harder to think of a limitless tomorrow. In its extreme, there seems little reason why a very aged person should take much interest in life. Yet, some manage to preserve the vital delusions, because of their deep involvement in the *process* of living.

Various religions have tried to offer balm in promises of an afterlife, thus supporting the delusion of immortality, by positing life in another form, full of the satisfactions one lacked in the first installment.

The great aristocratic dynasties tried to deal with problems of the disturbance of this delusion in their own way. Having a long family tree and expecting it to continue, lock, stock, and castle, was one way of seeing one's self-perpetuation. And if one could claim descent from a god, all the better. It makes one's existence part of a timeless chain.

The delusion of *unlimited possibilities* is closely interwoven with the idea of immortality. Both combine to make almost every youth feel superior to almost every older person, regardless of all other factors affecting their station in life. It is as if they were feeling, "That old codger" (who might be not more than thirty seen by a sixteen-year old) "has had it. There he is, but how far is that? Before me lies a world without limits—and he'll be dead long before I am." Seemingly unlimited time is an integral part of the apparently unlimited possibilities of youth. In fact, the end of youth could be defined as that point in life when the time before one seems no longer unlimited.

In a way, time itself is the most inexplicable of all personal experiences and a serious blow to the feeling of unlimited possibilities. To be the same as twenty years ago— and yet not the same—in feeling, in looks, and body—is constantly baffling. Imagine that you revisit the place of your birth and youth after an absence of twenty years. The house still stands, the door you passed through so many times is in front of you, and you relive a hundred happenings in a moment. It is you, the same fellow, but it is also not the boy who hurried in from the ball park to get to dinner on time, or the young man filled with mingled emotions after an eventful date. The children who crowd around you see you as a middleaged man and call you "Sir," while you can recall your being their age and pitching pennies in front of the same wall they're playing against now.

Time and place and you are in an elusive interplay. It confuses one's feeling of identity, and it eventually robs one of the feeling of unlimited possibilities. As the options decrease, unhappiness is bound to set in. The very healthy, as well as the most self-centered, may be spared this feeling because denial and repression work well for them. Others will go to great lengths to maintain their self-esteem. If their self image is impaired, they are reminded of their limitations. If a businessman cannot get preferential treatment in a restaurant, he shrinks like a punctured balloon.

Different people run into a limitation of their possibilities at different times. Some kill themselves in the attempt to prove that no limits of attainment exist for them.

There are great opportunities for achievement in contemporary society, especially the American one, and this results in an increased drive to achieve. In the caste-bound society of the East, in the rigidly-structured feudal society and the later class-structured system, there was hardly any reason for rushing. Everyone's place was well determined and, with few exceptions, most people's lives moved within predictable spheres. The limits of pleasure and activity were narrow even for the wellborn. Travel was occasional, the opportunities for varied experience numbered. One might as well have lingered where one was because there was no place to go. After all, had not God ordained one's place in life, with certain reward in the hereafter, if one suffered quietly and went along the predetermined path?

In today's culture, upward mobility is the rule. America still deserves to be known as the land of unlimited opportunity. Europe and other countries with expanding technologies are developing in the same image, but can still serve as contrasting examples in some ways. The European writer still does not have as easy access to a mass market as his American counterpart. The European scientist still has only relatively few positions and honors available, and the worker is still rather limited by narrow national boundaries. Therefore, the European writer may be more likely to linger over his work than the American who can count on a huge market and the best seller list if he is successful. TV and the movies not only hold unlimited lures, but constantly pressure him into reaching for farther horizons of attainment. The American scientist, the businessman, and the worker are not too differently situated.

The fact, then, is that our world of greater opportunities encourages the delusion of unlimited possibilities. With all sorts of chances dangling in front of one's eyes, it is easier to forget that there may be no tomorrow and that it might be wise to linger and enjoy. (Something in which Americans do not excel.)

Horace gave Leuconoe some good advice (even if it was just a lover's line to his restless mistress) : *carpe diem*— enjoy the day, make the most of what you have, because you cannot tell what else the gods have in store for you and me.

In that poem Horace combined an affirmation of life with an awareness of the delusion of unlimited possibilities. Of course, he was a lover not only of Leuconoe but of the grape, and made himself and his muse serve his lord and Caesar to attain a quiet country place for the enjoyment of both.

Unlike Horace's bucolia, a fellow who has to work

hard to sustain his belief in unlimited possibilities is the manic. By strenuous denial he believes in his inexhaustible capacities and magic powers. He is a caricature of all the rest of us. More than the average person he needs tremendous activity and a feeling of unlimited possibilities to cover up a sense of inadequacy, of disappointment with life. He tries to increase his low self-esteem by talking at tremendous speed about endless projects of great import and his own exalted status as moneymaker or statesman. He is only one step beyond the really big businessman who goes on piling million upon million for no demonstrable purpose. He could remind one of a president who needed a show of popularity ratings and control of every minute facet of power, while already being the most powerful man in the world.

The manic, the not quite manic, and all of us others often hide behind a great deal of noise and posturing the fact that we feel small and limited, and eventually limited by death.

There is the reason for the close alliance between the delusion of immortality and the delusion of unlimited possibilities: the ultimate limit of all possibilities lies in our mortality. Life is one experiment which cannot be repeated in another variation as scientists like to do in the laboratory. Limitation to a single run is dramatized in Hercules at the parting of the ways, in Caesar at the Rubicon, and Robert Frost in his poem, "Road Not Taken." Our limitations often hide in the little phrase, "If only I would have. . . ."

The delusion of *freedom of will* is important. It is vital for an endurable life to have the delusion, almost unconsciously, that at any moment one is the master of one's own destiny and not the product of glands, culture, the barometric pressure, genes, or the twentieth century.

This vital delusion is beautifully illustrated in the idea that all men are born free and equal. There is the conception that one starts as a clean slate, that one is omnivalent, unfettered by determining tendencies, ready to be molded only by oneself à la Horatio Alger, soaring to limitless heights.

To be "one's own man," unique unto oneself, is part of the quest for identity. To feel free, one seems to have to deny any dependent relationship, causal, genetic, ideational, or otherwise to anyone else. This paradox, as part of the fight for individuation, is at the root of the fights against the establishment. Beards and barricades, trips on pot and LSD, are part of the attempt of every young generation to proclaim its delusion of freedom from the fetters of the old and from the combining walls of reality.

The idea that we are activated by other than our own mind and other than free choice is felt as an indignity. For some, direction by divine power may seem like a desirable exception. Such divine direction is accepted as for the best. Self-determination is ceded to a better and all-knowing parental image.

In actual practice, the divinity and its designs are rarely more than a projection of one's own desires. In the First World War, each army was quite convinced that God was on *its* side. God is frequently simply implored to bless one's own decisions with success.

Subliminal advertising, "brain washing," and the Big Brother of 1984, on the other hand, are felt as a serious threat because they interfere with the feeling of personal freedom of choice which seems so vital.

The fact is that simple suggestions affect us all the time. Motivational market research foisted on us successfully such items as the hardtop car which looks like a convertible but isn't. It has us buying "Thunderbirds" and "Mustangs," makes you put "a tiger in your tank" and Hai Karate cologne on the male face, and the promise of "Je Reviens" on the female one. Yet, we like to preserve the feeling that we exercise freedom of action and thought.

Riesman spoke of the outer-directed "lonely" crowd as having all its choices determined by the Joneses. The inner-directed man has built-in, tradition-oriented cultural values which afford delusions of absolute personal standards. These values serve him like a built-in gyroscope that makes him fly level. His selective inattentiveness is well functioning. Identifying with his parents and his teachers, he has internalized certain cultural norms and cues for perceiving and not perceiving.

Valuable as such inner-direction may be for a man's emotional stability in terms of standards unswayed by the Joneses and fashion rages, he is also in danger of being the fossilized man of the establishment. He can all too easily utilize the vital delusions and his selective inattentiveness for inappropriately preserving the status quo. The delusion of timelessness preserves him from a sense of hurry in changing the lot of the underprivileged. The delusion of freedom of will and unlimited possibility is vitally necessary for him to maintain a sense of well being. The belief in a freedom of will has permitted some smug people to feel secure in the notion that the poor deserve their lot because they did not try hard enough to exercise their freedom of action to take advantage of the unlimited possibilities life holds for every rightminded person.

The delusion of free will is susceptible to cultural influence. In nations which have a history of thousands of years of oppression, like India and China, fatalism takes the place of self determination. It is as if helplessness against famine, illness, and oppressors makes abdication of most personal direction a more vital delusion than freedom of will. Allah's will, the caste system, transmigration of the soul, and some sort of compensatory heaven take the place of self determination.

Freedom of will, along with its political form, democracy, may be the offspring of a state of plenty. First raised in ancient Greece's well-to-do city states, it was submerged in the economic-theological mire of the Middle Ages. It raised its head again with the rise of commerce, notably in England with its mother of Parliaments. As long as workers were disenfranchised, they were not much different from the helpless masses of the Far East. Marx himself said that no revolt, not even resentment against their oppressors, could be expected from the "Lumpen proletariat," the abysmally poor.

The delusion of freedom of will reached its peak in the United States some years ago. Economic freedom led to a denial of any limitations. We have turned the corner, however, by courtesy of the A- and H-bombs. Modern youth's flight to gurus and intoxicating drugs is perhaps the direct outcome of their despair over being unable to control their destiny. It is impossible to preserve delusions of immortality in the omnipresence of the H-bomb.

It is hard to feel oneself full of unlimited possibilities in a well-regulated welfare state. It is difficult to believe in freedom of will in a world controlled by mass media. The establishment's vital delusions fail to work for a youth frightened by many wars, disillusioned by nationalism, and devoid of stable standards. The life of the hippies is as irrationally fatalistic and passive as the Indian masses used to be.

Salvation must lie somewhere between smug reliance on vital delusions supported by dangerously selective attention and an irrational discarding of all values with a flight into irrational passivity.

Underlying both extremes of behavior is really a *fourth delusion*, the most dangerous of all: that there is a *perfect way*, an *attainable state of bliss*, an ultimate truth to be had, either as a proper member of the establishment with intact delusions of one's power or as passive flotsam in the world of some god or nirvana.

For adolescent girls and grown-up dreamers, Hollywood is a state of bliss. The Burton-Taylor marriage is a piece of heaven to them. To the businessman, Valhalla is getting to the million or the 100 million mark. To Rousseau, the noble savage was an idyllic figure, and to the tired Madison Avenue man, beachcombing sounds like a blissful getting away from it all.

The truth is that there is no assured state of bliss that can be an end in itself. Work, striving, and love cannot serve primarily for attainment of an end but for their own sake, the process as an end in itself, within the rules of the game.

Therefore, happiness is built on a paradox. It seems

logically true that life is senseless in terms of a specific goal, *except for the one of being a well-lived life*. To live a happy life it is necessary not to be aware most of the time that there are no absolute goals to be achieved, but to enjoy the art of striving toward them.

Probably the best chance for a relatively happy life lies in enjoyment of the act of living, not crudely and hedonistically, but as a responsible social being. The curious fact is that this process of absorption with others lifts the oppression of self absorption.

Happiness lies in a good deal of detour behavior, of self negation, or at least of negation of immediate drive gratification. It sounds uncomfortably like religious exhortation and yet seems clinical fact. Feats of sexual athletes offer only shallow gratification. A man successful in the entertainment industry often made love to two or three different beautiful girls a day. If it ever did him any good one failed to notice it. He still felt a failure and needed a handful of pep pills not to be too depressed. Whether one likes it or not, one gets about as much deep pleasure from a sexual act or from work as the effort one puts into it. Self-absorption and self-gratification usually lead to a feeling of aloneness that makes everything useless.

It is the misfortune of the neurotic not to have stable relations with others and, thus, to suffer in a multitude of ways as the vital delusions fail. Existential philosophy has made this fact a central part of its tenets; existential psychology has oversimplified and romanticized it. For the fact is that this disturbance in relations to others is not of one amorphous general nature, but of many subtle, distinct variations which need to be understood technically and skillfully reversed in terms of the many hypotheses of classical psychoanalysis.

Schopenhauer was quite right. The will, the need, the drive, is blind and by itself is not rational for the individual. Rather than negating the drive, psychoanalysis hopes that one may maintain a stable drive gratification which carries in its own activity the nature of gratification.

Vita gratia vitae. Life is its own reward. In that case there is no hunting for greener fields because gratification lies in working the fields one has. One can stabilize one's drives and emotions to the point where the means become an end in itself. The alternative is to continuously drive for some end as another means to more, greater, bigger, better—and no place at all.

Goethe treated this theme in *Faust*. The restless human spirit whom Faust represents par excellence has studied medicine, philosophy, theology, and jurisprudence in an effort to find happiness, but without success. He is even willing to offer his soul to the Devil for a moment of happiness. As we know, in the end Goethe found redemption for Faust only in finding work an end in itself. It took Goethe many decades to write *Faust*; he was a very old man before his protagonist came to rest. It could be that the ebbing energies of old age make it more palatable to accept the means as an end in itself.